THE DARK SIDE OF GREEN

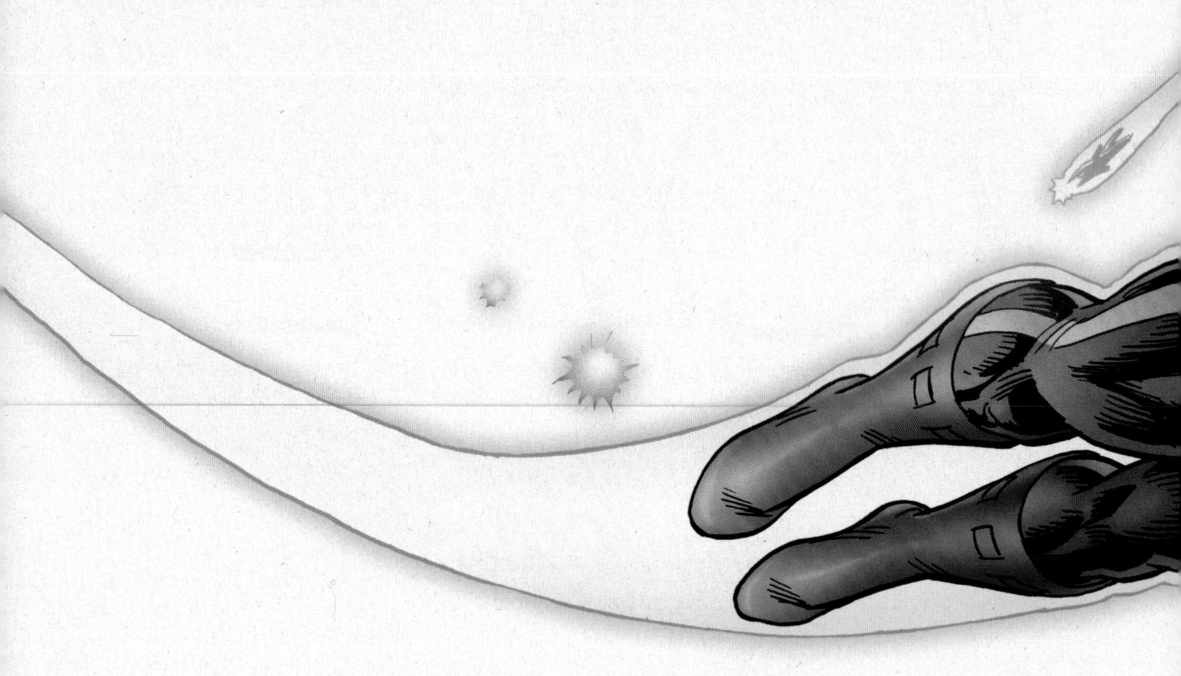

Cover art by Patrick Gleason,
Tom Nguyen and Moose Baumann

GREEN LANTERN CORPS:
THE DARK SIDE OF GREEN
Published by DC Comics.

DC Comics, 1700 Broadway, New York, NY 10019
A Warner Bros. Entertainment Company
Printed in Canada. Second Printing.

ISBN: 978-1-4012-1507-1

THE DARK SIDE OF GREEN

Dave Gibbons
Keith Champagne
Writers

Patrick Gleason
Dave Gibbons
Tom Nguyen
Pencils

Prentis Rollins
Ray Snyder
Christian Alamy
Inks

Phil Balsman
Letters

Moose Baumann
Colors

GREEN LANTERN CORPS #7
Cover by Patrick Gleason, Wayne Faucher and Moose Baumann

IT BURNS AT YOU STILL, EVEN ALL THESE ROTATIONS PAST.
I KNOW THIS IS TRUE BECAUSE I FEEL IT TOO, SEARING AT THE CORE OF MY BEING.
IT IS THE HEAT OF OUR ANGER. OUR FURY. OUR HATRED.
OUR SHAME AT BEING...
...DEFEATED.
EARTH.
THE WORD ITSELF TASTES LIKE A BLADE.
TO HAVE OUR GRAND INVASION TURNED BACK BY SUCH AN INSIGNIFICANT BALL OF MUD...
TO THIS DAY, THE UNIVERSE SECRETLY LAUGHS BEHIND THE BACKS OF THE DOMINATORS.
OUR REVENGE IS LONG PAST DUE.
NOT REVENGE. REDEMPTION.
THERE WILL BE NO ERROR IN OUR SECOND ATTEMPT, NO FAILURE. THERE SHALL ONLY BE VICTORY. AT LONG LAST, OUR SOULS WILL KNOW PEACE.
ALL THANKS TO MY TIRELESS EFFORTS.
MY DISCOVERY.
TELL ME, CASTE LEADERS.. WOULD YOU LIKE TO HEAR MORE?

YOU MAY PROCEED.
LIMIT YOUR ORATION TO YOUR DISCOVERIES. YOUR TRANSPARENT THEATRICS TRY OUR PATIENCE.
AS THAT PATIENCE NEARS ITS END, SO DOES YOUR EXISTENCE.
YES...
...OF COURSE, CASTE LEADERS. MY MOST HUMBLE APOLOGIES.
IF IT SUITS YOU, PLEASE...TURN AROUND.
INTERESTING.

YOUR WORK SHOWS POTENTIAL.
AARRH!
THE DARK SIDE OF GREEN
PART ONE
KEITH CHAMPAGNE writer PATRICK GLEASON penciller PRENTIS ROLLINS inker
MOOSE BAUMANN colorist PHIL BALSMAN letterer

GOTTA SAY, THE GUARDIANS ARE REALLY PUTTIN' THE GREEN IN THE CORPS WITH YOU NEW RECRUITS.

A WEEK OUT OF BASIC AND YOU'RE ALREADY IN THE FIELD. I MUST HAVE BAD KARMA.
LUCKY FOR YOU, I'M A HELL OF A LEAD. ANY PROBLEMS ON THIS RUN, JUST SIT BACK. GUY GARDNER WILL SHOW YOU HOW TO TANGO.

SO...WHERE YOU FROM AGAIN? RING, REFRESH MY MEMORY.
CORPSMAN R'AMEY HOLL. RACE: MONARCHIST. HOME PLANET: PAPILLIOX.

PAPILLIOX. HUH?
NEVER HEARD OF THAT ONE. THEY GOT NICE BEACHES?

THEY ALL AS QUIET AS YOU ON PAPILLI-WHATEVER? IF I WAS THE INSECURE TYPE, I MIGHT THINK YOU DIDN'T LIKE ME.
I KNOW, I KNOW...CRAZY TALK. WHAT CAN I SAY?

I ALWAYS GO STIR CRAZY ON THESE LONG TRIPS THROUGH HYPERSPACE.
I'VE HAD EASIER TIMES JAWIN' WITH THE BAT.

CAN'T BEAT THAT VIEW THOUGH.
APPROACHING CORONA SEVEN.
WERE YOU SPEAKING, SENIOR CORPSMAN GARDNER? MY MIND VANISH-WRAPPED IN THE RHYTHM-POETRY OF HYPER TRAVEL.
I WAS SAYIN'-- QUIT YOUR DAYDREAMING AND GET READY TO DROP OUT OF WARP. RING SAYS WE'RE HERE.

CORONA SEVEN. CURRENT TEMPERATURE: MINUS TWO HUNDRED FORTY DEGREES. ORGANIC LIFE: NIL.
POP QUIZ, ROOKIE. THE GUARDIANS HAVE SENT YOU TO THE ICIEST CORNER OF THE UNIVERSE TO DELIVER A MESSAGE TO SOME JOKER NAMED VON DAGGLE.
YOU GET THERE AND THE RING SAYS NOBODY'S HOME. WHAT'S YOUR NEXT MOVE, TOOTS?
REGULATIONS SUGGEST-DICTATE THAT CORPSMEN CONTACT OA FOR ADDITIONAL ASSISTANCE-INSTRUCTION.
SURE THING...IF YOU WANT TO BE A KISS-ASS. YOU LOOKING TO BE A GREEN LANTERN, TRY AND KEEP UP. CLASS IS NOW IN SESSION.
I BEEN SLINGIN' THE GREEN FOR A LONG TIME, SO LET ME CLUE YOU IN ON SOMETHIN' I LEARNED OVER THE YEARS.
THE LITTLE BLUE MUNCHKINS AIN'T ALWAYS RIGHT--BUT THEY'RE ALWAYS RIGHT. COMPRENDE?
I DO NOT COMPREHEND-UNDERSTAND.
LET ME BREAK IT DOWN REAL SIMPLE. IF THE GUARDIANS SAY THIS DAGGLE FELLA IS ON CORONA SEVEN, TRUST ME, HE'S SOMEWHERE ON CORONA SEVEN.
HOPE YOU BROUGHT SNOWSHOES. WE AIN'T LEAVING UNTIL WE FIND HIM.

DON'T KNOW ABOUT YOU, BUT IF I LIVED ON A BALL OF ICE, I MIGHT GO DEEP UNDERGROUND. TRY AND GET AWAY FROM THE COLD AND SHRINKAGE.
MAYBE OUT OF SCANNING RANGE, TOO.

SENIOR CORPSMAN, I SCENT-DETECT SOMETHING...

...SOMETHING GRAY.
NOW THAT'S WHAT I'M TALKIN' ABOUT. WHERE THERE'S SMOKE, THERE'S FIRE. WHERE THERE'S FIRE, THERE'S LIFE.
LET'S TAKE A PEEK. NICE AND EASY, SHIELDS UP.

SENIOR CORPSMAN, A MOMENT-WORD.
MY TIME-DAYS IN THE CORPS MAY BE BRIEF, BUT MY LAW-SERVICE ON PAPILLIOX IS VAST-SPANNING.
I AM NO INFANT-NOVICE. DO NOT TREAT ME AS SUCH.

HEH.
I THINK MY NIPPLES JUST GOT HARD.

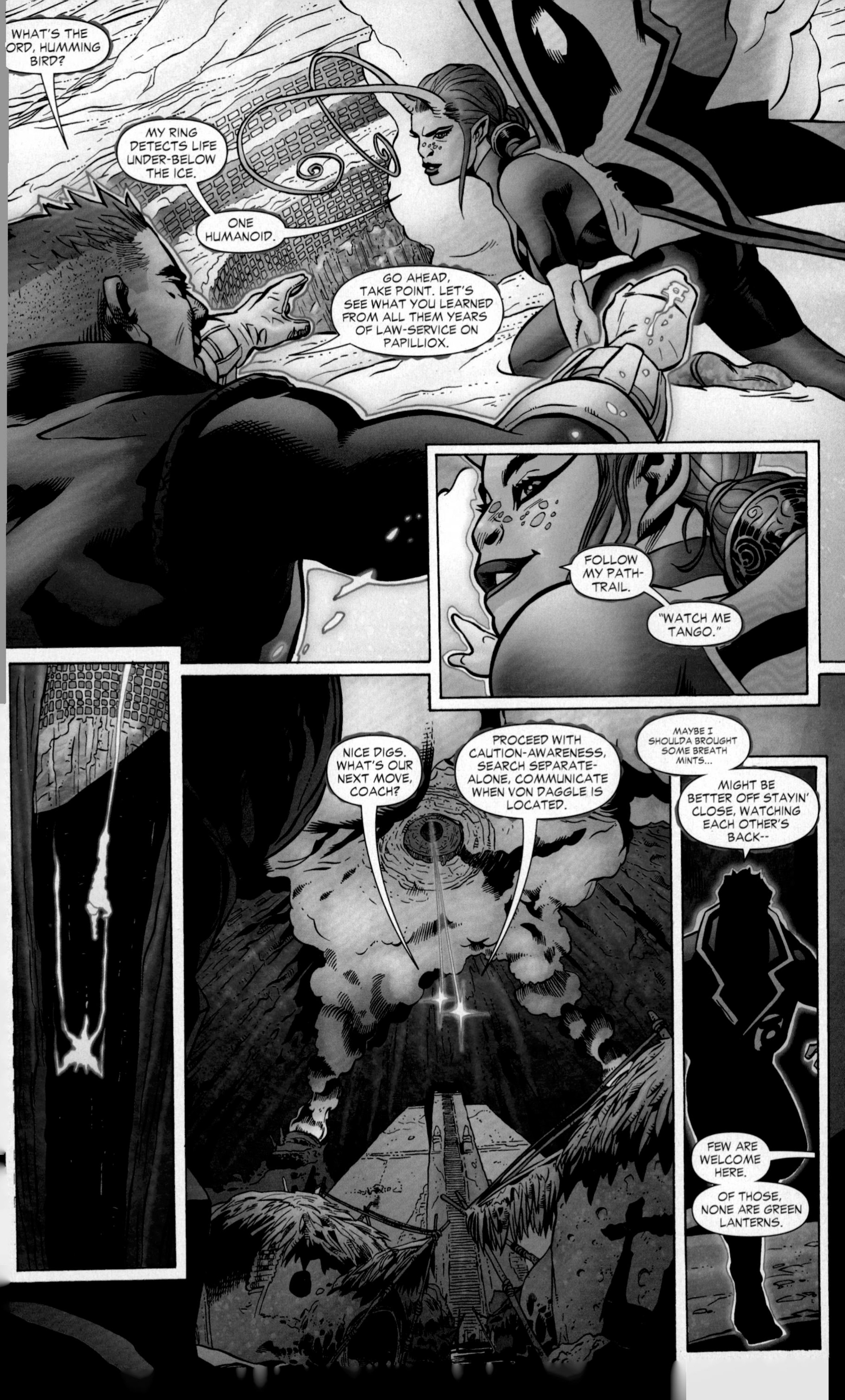
WHAT'S THE ORD, HUMMING BIRD?
MY RING DETECTS LIFE UNDER-BELOW THE ICE.
ONE HUMANOID.
GO AHEAD, TAKE POINT. LET'S SEE WHAT YOU LEARNED FROM ALL THEM YEARS OF LAW-SERVICE ON PAPILLIOX.
FOLLOW MY PATH-TRAIL.
"WATCH ME TANGO."
NICE DIGS. WHAT'S OUR NEXT MOVE, COACH?
PROCEED WITH CAUTION-AWARENESS, SEARCH SEPARATE-ALONE, COMMUNICATE WHEN VON DAGGLE IS LOCATED.
MAYBE I SHOULDA BROUGHT SOME BREATH MINTS...
MIGHT BE BETTER OFF STAYIN' CLOSE, WATCHING EACH OTHER'S BACK--
FEW ARE WELCOME HERE.
OF THOSE, NONE ARE GREEN LANTERNS.

THERE'S HALF OF A MESSAGE ENCODED IN THIS RING, THE OTHER HALF IN YOURS.
THAT'S THE GUARDIANS' WAY OF KEEPING IT OUT OF THE WRONG HANDS.
IF YOU'RE WONDERING WHO I AM AND HOW I KNOW THIS, IT'S BECAUSE I WAS VERY GOOD AT MY JOB.
PAST TENSE. I LOST TOO MANY GOOD MEN WHEN THE GUARDIANS' HOUSE OF CARDS COLLAPSED.
SO GO BACK TO OA AND TELL THEM THAT VON DAGGLE ISN'T INTERESTED.
DON'T COME BACK. I WON'T BE SUCH A GENTLEMAN NEXT TIME.
YOU GOT SOME KINDA BEEF WITH THE GUARDIANS, THAT AIN'T MY CROSS TO BEAR.
START SHOOTING MESSENGERS AND SUDDENLY WE GOT A PROBLEM.
BECAUSE YOU'RE A DURLAN, I'LL USE SMALL WORDS.
YOU GOT THREE SECONDS TO DROP THAT RING AND BACK THE HELL AWAY FROM MY PARTNER.
THREE...
...TWO...
ZZZAK
SKRASH
ONE.
RAAAAAAAAGH!

OOH, SCARY. A DURLAN CHANGES SHAPE INTO A FEROCIOUS BEAST.
NEVER SAW THAT ONE BEFORE.

HUH?

ACK!

HRRRK... GIIH... UHCK--

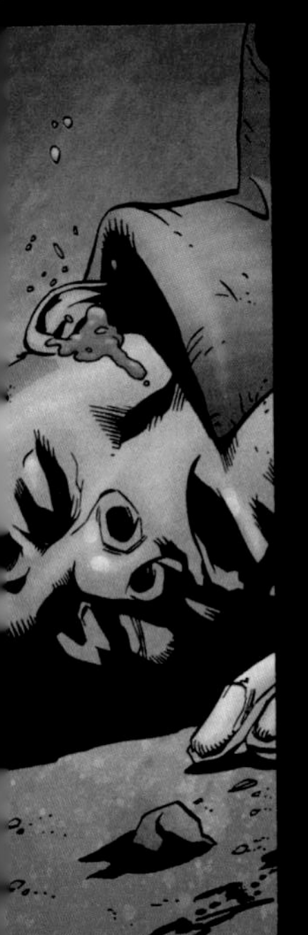

THE ASTEROID IS THE KEY. IT WAS TAKEN FROM THE TAIL END OF A COMET AND GIVES OFF A SINGULARLY UNIQUE FORM OF **RADIATION**.

TO THE BEST OF OUR KNOWLEDGE, INDIVIDUALS FROM COUNTLESS RACES AND PLANETS HAVE BEEN GIFTED BY THIS ANOMALY.

THIS RADIATION SOMEHOW **EVOLVES** THOSE IT COMES INTO CONTACT WITH. IT RAISES THEM TO THE PEAK OF THEIR NATURAL EVOLUTION.

THOSE EXPOSED TO IT OFTEN GAIN STAGGERING PHYSICAL AND MENTAL ABILITIES.

ON **EARTH**, IT CREATED THE META-HUMAN KNOWN AS CAPTAIN COMET.

TAKES YOUR BREATH AWAY, DOESN'T IT?

THE ONLY SETBACK MY RESEARCH ENCOUNTERED WAS RELATED TO THE LIMITATIONS OF THE KHUNDIAN **BRAIN**.
EVEN EVOLVED TO ITS HIGHEST STATE, IT IS TOO **SMALL** TO SIMULTANEOUSLY PROCESS BOTH OCULAR AND **TELEPATHIC** INFORMATION.

A PROBLEM **EASILY** REMEDIED BY SIMPLY REMOVING HIS **EYES**.

BRUTALLY APPARENT.
AN ARMY OF KHUNDS SUCH AS THIS AT OUR DISPOSAL...IT'S ENOUGH TO MAKE ME DROOL.
HOW TO CONTROL SUCH A BEAST, THOUGH?
A BIOLOGICAL KILL SWITCH COULD BE IMPLANTED.
WOULD DO NICELY.
CASTE LEADERS, PLEASE. THIS KHUND WAS CREATED TO SERVE AS AN EXAMPLE: TO DEMONSTRATE THE POSSIBILITIES.
MY INTENT WAS TO CREATE A NEW RACE OF EVOLVED DOMINATORS. NO LONGER WOULD WE RELY ON THE LESSER RACES. WE WOULD BE FREE FROM THEIR FAILINGS.
YOUR WORK WILL PROVE USEFUL TO THE DOMINION AND SO YOUR LIFE WILL BE SPARED. YOU WILL IMMEDIATELY CEASE THIS TALK.
PERFECTION CANNOT EVOLVE. THE DOMINATORS ARE ALREADY THE PINNACLE OF CREATION. YOU SPEAK HERESY.
IN RETURN FOR YOUR LIFE, YOU WILL TURN YOUR RESEARCH AND EQUIPMENT OVER TO US.
OUR WISDOM SHALL PERFECT THIS PROCESS. WE WILL USE IT TO CREATE AN ARMY OF KHUNDS.
COME. LET US BEGIN TO DESIGN THE KILL SWITCH.

CORONA SEVEN.

AHHH!

S-SOUND OFF, K-KID. STILL... STILL WITH M-ME?
MY LIFE...FLICKER-DIMS, SENIOR CORPSMAN GUY...

B-BASTARD TOOK OUR R-RINGS, DUMPED US OUT HERE T-TO DIE.
CAN'T S-SEE FOR NOTHIN' B-BUT...THAT V-VENT...C-CAN'T BE F-FAR.

P-PULL IT T-TOGETHER, KID. YOU G-GOTTA SNIFF IT O-OUT AGAIN.
WE'RE N-NOT G-GONNA LAST AN HOUR O-OUT HERE. Y-YOU LISTENING, K-KID?

CRAP.
FUMP

T-TOUGH L-L-LOVE IT IS...

C-CAN'T STAND T-THE COLD? T-THAT'S 'CAUSE IT **BLOWS.** DON'T GIVE YOU THE RIGHT TO J-JUST LAY D-DOWN A-AND DIE!
Y-YOU WANTED T-TO BE A **GREEN LANTERN?** TH-**THIS** IS WHAT THE J-JOB **IS.** IT'S **COLD** AND HARD AND C-CAN BEAT YA HALF TO D-DEATH.

C-CAN'T HACK IT, YOU SHOULD'A S-STAYED ON BUTTERFLY W-WORLD.

O-ON YOUR **FEET,** ROOKIE! MY M-MOTHER DIDN'T R-RAISE M-ME TO END UP A P-**POPSICLE.**
BESIDES, W-WE G-GOT SOME DURLAN ASS T-TO KICK.

SLAP
R'AMEY!!
T-TIME TO PUNCH THE C-CLOCK!!

...C'MON, KID...CAN'T D-DO THIS WITHOUT YOU.

FAP

THAT'S WHAT I'M TALKIN' ABOUT!!
THE GRAY-SCENT LIES TOWARD THE WEST.
THIS WHITE-COLD IS FOREIGN-ALIEN ON PAPILLIOX. IT IS... UNBEARABLE.
H-HANG IN THERE, KID. YOU'RE D-DOING GREAT.
Whoo--

--OOAAAAAAAAH!!
KID, YOU GOTTA PULL UP, WE'RE GONNA--
KRASH
MY REGRET-APOLOGIES, CORPSMAN GUY. OUR TUMBLE-LANDING WAS PAINFUL.
NAH, YOU DONE GREAT, KID.
SOME JOKER BACK ON EARTH COINED A PHRASE ONCE. ACCORDING TO HIM, ANY LANDING YOU CAN WALK AWAY FROM IS A GOOD ONE.
REMIND ME TO KICK THAT GUY'S ASS IF I EVER SEE HIM.
DON'T LISTEN TO ME, I'M JUST A LITTLE PISSED OFF. NOTHING STOMPIN' A HOLE THROUGH A DURLAN WON'T FIX.
REST FOR A SPELL. I'LL FIND DAGGLE AND GET OUR RINGS BACK.

DAGGLE.
THOUGHT ABOUT CREEPIN' UP ON YOU, THEN I REMEMBERED BEING SNEAKY IS MORE YOUR KIND OF THING.
THIS IS HOW I ROLL!
KRAK
WHA--!!

R'AMEY!
HOW THE HELL?!!?
THE GUARDIANS ARE SLIPPING, SENDING MEAT LIKE YOU TO FIND ME.
YOU'RE STRONG AS AN ANDUVIAN BULLCRAB BUT A GALAXY COULD FIT IN THAT SPACE BETWEEN YOUR EARS.
WITH ROOM LEFT OVER FOR A FEW EXTRA PLANETS.
IF YOU CAN'T TAKE A SECOND TO STOP AND THINK, YOU'RE USELESS TO ME.
TO THE MISSION.
IT WAS YOU ON THE SURFACE. YOU WANT TO PLAY GAMES, PAL, MAYBE I BETTER TEACH YOU THE RULES.
HAD TO SEE WHAT YOU'RE MADE OF, CORPSMAN.
THE MONARCHIST MIGHT BE NEW, BUT THERE'S A REASON THE GUARDIANS SENT HER. SOME OF MY BEST MEN WERE FROM PAPILLIOX.
HUMANS THOUGH... YOU'RE A CONFLICTED BUNCH.
I DON'T TRUST YOUR KIND.
TAKE YOUR TRINKETS BACK. SYNCH UP AND VIEW THE GUARDIANS' MESSAGE.
I CHECKED IT OUT WHILE THE TWO OF YOU WERE SLEEPING. YOU MIGHT FIND IT ILLUMINATING.
FIND ME WHEN YOU'RE UP TO SPEED AND WE'LL GO FROM THERE.

RING, GIMME A STATUS REPORT.
ENERGY LEVEL: 43%. WAITING TO SYNCH.
SORRY ABOUT THAT, KID. HATE TO SAY IT, BUT OUR BOY DAGGLE PUT ONE OVER ON ME BUT GOOD.
HOPE YOUR SKULL AIN'T RINGING TOO LOUD.
I'VE BEEN STRUCK-ENDURED FAR WORSE. RING, SYSTEM-GREEN LEVELS?
GREEN LEVELS: MODERATE. MERGE-VIEW PENDING.
BEGIN-INITIATE, SENIOR CORPSMAN GUY?
IF THAT MEANS HITTING THE PLAY BUTTON, LET'S DO IT. I'M SICK OF BEING YANKED AROUND.
VON DAGGLE.
FOR YEARS, YOU AND YOUR MEN SECRETLY WORKED IN THE SHADOWS OF THE UNIVERSE.
YOU SERVED OA LOYALLY, WITHOUT FEAR OR HESITATION, NO MATTER HOW DARK THE TASK.

THE CORPS HAS BEEN REBORN.

ONCE MORE, YOU ARE ALSO CALLED BACK INTO SERVICE.

THE DOMINATORS HAVE TAKEN POSSESSION OF AN ANCIENT ARTIFACT. THEIR MINDS ARE TOO SMALL TO UNDERSTAND THE TRUE NATURE OF ITS POWER. THEY SEE ONLY A ***WEAPON.***

IN FACT, IT SHALL PROVE TO BE THE ***END*** OF THEIR WORLD. BILLIONS OF LIVES WILL BE LOST.

THE DOMINATORS SERVE A VALUABLE ROLE IN THIS UNIVERSE. THEY MUST BE SAVED, EVEN FROM THEMSELVES.

I GIVE YOU THESE TWO CORPSMEN, GUY GARDNER OF EARTH AND R'AMEY HOLL OF PAPILLIOX, TO AID YOU. THEY ARE THE FIRST RECRUITS SUPPLIED TO REBUILD YOUR DIVISION.

GO TO THE DOMINION HOME WORLD AND TAKE POSSESSION OF THE ARTIFACT.

VON DAGGLE, MUCH TIME HAS PASSED. YOU MAY NO LONGER BE WILLING TO SHOULDER YOUR RESPONSIBILITIES, TO FULFILL THE ***OATH*** YOU ONCE TOOK.

OF THIS, I CAN ONLY SAY: HELP US AGAIN AND WE WILL HELP ***YOU.*** WE KNOW WHERE ***SHE*** IS.

FAILURE IS NOT AN OPTION.

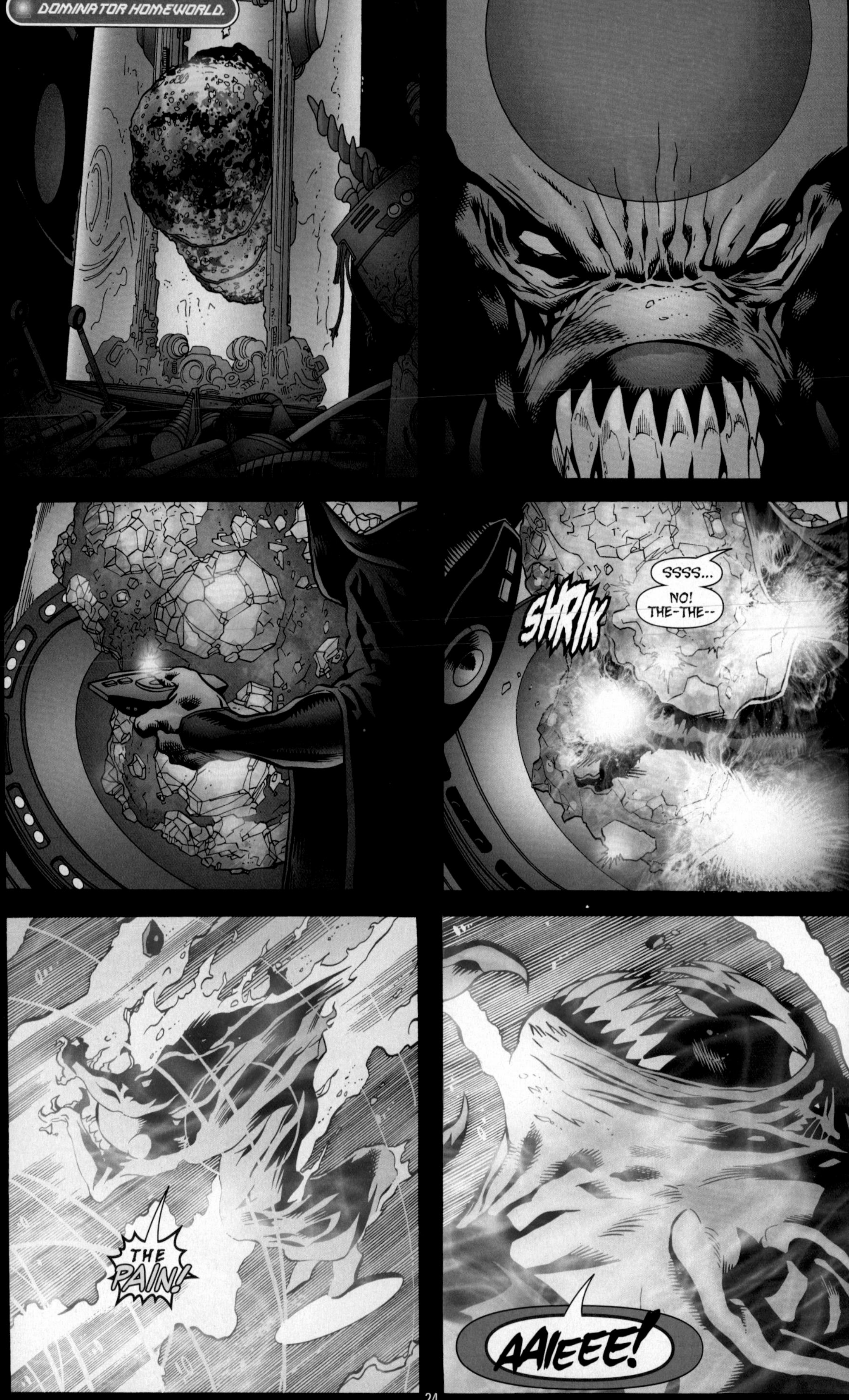
DOMINATOR HOMEWORLD.
SHRIK
SSSS...
NO! THE-THE--
THE PAIN!
AAIEEE!

WE GOTTA SAVE THOSE CREEPY YELLOW BASTARDS, THAT'S ONE THING BUT--
DITCH YOUR UNIFORMS AND GET RID OF THOSE RINGS. THEY'RE TOO OBVIOUS.
WE WORK UNDER DEEP COVER, NO TIES TO OA OR THE CORPS. IF WE'RE CAPTURED, NO ONE'S COMING TO SAVE US.
THESE CAME WITH THE GUARDIANS' MESSAGE, ONE FOR EACH OF US.
TAKE ONE AND SWALLOW IT. THEY WORK THE SAME AS YOUR RINGS. CHARGE LASTS THE EQUIVALENT OF FIVE DAYS, EARTH TIME.
IF WE'RE NOT OUT BY THEN, WE DON'T GET OUT.
ENOUGH IS ENOUGH. WHAT THE HELL IS GOING ON?
I WANT ANSWERS AND I WANT THEM--
THERE'S A TIME AND A PLACE, GARDNER. FOR NOW, HERE'S WHAT YOU NEED TO KNOW...

YOU'VE JUST BEEN INDUCTED INTO THE COLDEST, HARDEST, MEANEST DIVISION OF THE GREEN LANTERN CORPS YOU NEVER EVEN KNEW EXISTED.
CAN'T HANDLE IT? TOUGH LUCK, YOU DON'T HAVE A CHOICE.
WE LIVE IN THE PLACES THAT ARE TOO DARK FOR THE LIGHT OF THE CORPS.
WE HANDLE THE JOBS THAT ARE TOO DIRTY FOR THE GREEN.
WELCOME TO THE CORPSE, LANTERNS.
STAY ALIVE LONG ENOUGH, YOU MIGHT JUST SAVE THE UNIVERSE.

GREEN LANTERN CORPS #[illegible]
Cover by Patrick Gleason, Wayne Faucher and Moose Baumann

PLEASURE.
WOULDN'T YOU AGREE, CASTE LEADERS?
THE CLEVERNESS OF OUR MACHINATIONS... ALMOST NOTHING BRINGS SUCH A STRONG SENSE OF--
JUSTIFICATION.
ALL RESEARCH CONDUCTED BY OUR LEAVE, BY NATURE OF ITS VERY EXISTENCE, RIGHTFULLY BELONGS TO US.
STILL, THE LOOK IN THE FOOL'S EYES WAS--
PRICELESS.
HE ACTUALLY BELIEVED HE WOULD BE REWARDED FOR HIS WORK. HIS STUPIDITY IS ENOUGH TO MAKE ME ASHAMED OF BEING A DOMINATOR.

THE SCIENTIST STILL BREATHES--UNTIL HIS WORK BECOMES OURS, AT LEAST. THAT IS HIS REWARD.
HOW TO DISPOSE OF HIM IN THE CRUELEST WAY POSSIBLE?
SIMPLE. THE MUTATED KHUND BELOW HUNGERS FOR FRESH--

MEAT.
IT SHALL **FEAST** TONIGHT, CASTE LEADERS. JUST NOT ON THE MEAL **YOU** INTENDED.

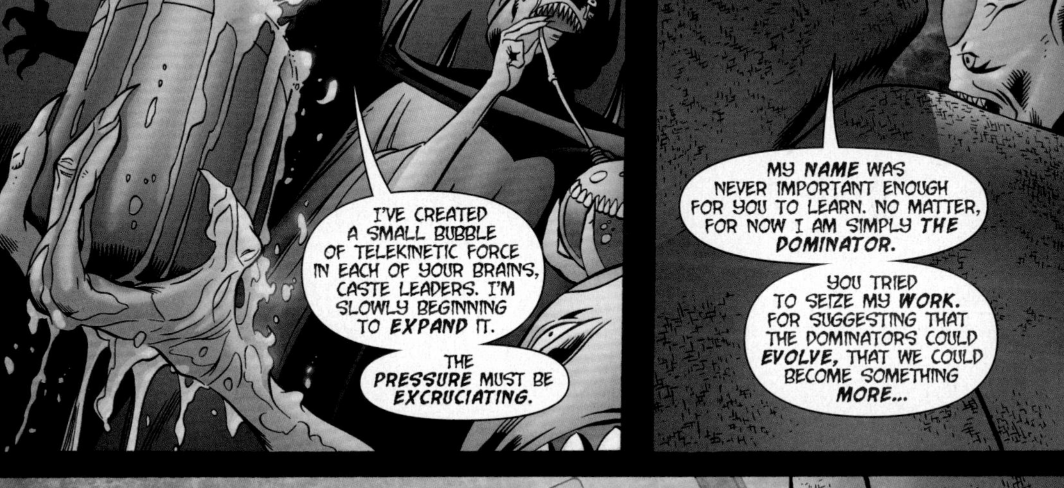
I'VE CREATED A SMALL BUBBLE OF TELEKINETIC FORCE IN EACH OF YOUR BRAINS, CASTE LEADERS. I'M SLOWLY BEGINNING TO **EXPAND** IT.
THE **PRESSURE** MUST BE **EXCRUCIATING**.
MY **NAME** WAS NEVER IMPORTANT ENOUGH FOR YOU TO LEARN. NO MATTER, FOR NOW I AM SIMPLY **THE DOMINATOR**.
YOU TRIED TO SEIZE MY **WORK**. FOR SUGGESTING THAT THE DOMINATORS COULD **EVOLVE**, THAT WE COULD BECOME SOMETHING **MORE...**

...YOU BRANDED ME A **HERETIC**.

HAVING TROUBLE CONCENTRATING, CASTE LEADERS?

THE DARK SIDE OF GREEN

PART TWO

KEITH CHAMPAGNE writer PATRICK GLEASON penciller
PRENTIS ROLLINS inker MOOSE BAUMANN colorist PHIL BALSMAN letterer

SIMULTANEOUSLY, IN A HOLDING CELL FAR BELOW ON DOMINION WORLD.
I KNOW YOU'RE THERE, MEAT. WATCHING, TRYING TO MASK YOUR BREATHING.
EVEN IF I WASN'T ABLE TO HEAR YOUR THOUGHTS, I COULD STILL SMELL YOU.
I KNOW WHAT YOU WANT.
I PLUCKED IT FROM YOUR HEAD WHILE YOUR THOUGHTS WANDERED.
THAT SHARP PAIN YOU FELT A FEW MOMENTS AGO?
I WANTED YOU TO NOTICE AS I ERASED YOUR MEMORIES OF YOUR MOTHER.
THEY WERE DELICIOUS.
DURLAN.
KILL YOU SOON.

MAYBE THERE'S NO AIR IN SPACE, BUT SOMETHING STILL SMELLS ROTTEN.
I BEEN IN THE CORPS LONGER THAN MOST AND I AIN'T NEVER HEARD OF NO SPECIAL DIVISION. SO YOU CAN COLOR ME SKEPTICAL, R'AMEY.
IF THIS CORPSE CRAP WERE AROUND AS LONG AS DAGGLE SAYS, SOMEONE WOULD HAVE SPILLED THE BEANS. PEOPLE LOVE TO FLAP THEIR GUMS.
I AIN'T NO TRAINED MONKEY WITH A RING, WIND ME UP, POINT AND SHOOT. NO WAY.
KNOW WHAT ELSE? I THINK THAT DURLAN IS A DAMN--
SENIOR CORPSMAN GARDNER?
YOU THINK-WORRY TOO MUCH.

NOT THAT I'M COMPLAINING, BUT...WHAT THE HELL WAS--
HATE TO SPOIL THIS MAGIC MOMENT, BUT LAST TIME I CHECKED WE WERE ON THE CLOCK.
BACK FROM YOUR COSTUME PARTY, DAGGLE?
LEARNING CURVE ON THIS IS SO STEEP IT'S TREACHEROUS. SO PUT YOUR HORMONES AWAY AND LISTEN TIGHT.
IT'S TOO QUIET DOWN THERE. NO ONE'S TALKING AND THAT MAKES ME NERVOUS.
EITHER EVERYONE'S CLUELESS OR THEY'RE ALL AFRAID TO SPEAK.
I FOUND A KHUND BEING HELD CAPTIVE IN ONE OF THE LOWER LEVELS OF THE CAPITAL.
HE'S... DIFFERENT.
FOR ONE, HE'S EVEN UGLIER THAN A NORMAL KHUND. SECOND, HE'S A MIND READER AND THAT'S PROBABLY NOT ALL

GOOD NEWS IS, HE'S STILL NEW AT PLAYING MIND GAMES.
HE'S SLOPPY. WHILE HE WAS WALKING THROUGH MY HEAD, I MANAGED TO FOLLOW HIS TRAIN OF THOUGHT BACK INTO HIS.
THIS ARTIFACT WE'RE HERE TO GRAB IS A CHUNK OF SPACE ROCK WITH A UNIQUE ENERGY SIGNATURE. IT SHOULD BE EASY TO TRACK DOWN.
R'AMEY HOLL, YOU'RE WITH ME ON THAT.
BAD NEWS IS, OUR PRESENCE HERE IS ALREADY COMPROMISED.
GARDNER, YOU'VE GOT SOME LIGHT-YEARS UNDER YOUR BELT. I'M GIVING YOU THE KHUND. THE MORE HE TALKS, THE HARDER OUR JOB BECOMES.
SHUT HIM UP.
...RIGHT...
WE'RE ON OUR OWN HERE, PEOPLE. IF WE GET CAUGHT IN THE FIRE, WE DIE LONELY. ALL WE HAVE TO DEPEND ON IS ONE ANOTHER.
EVERYONE DOES THEIR JOB AND WE ALL SEE TOMORROW. THIS IS ABOUT LOYALTY TO EACH OTHER AND DUTY TO THE GREATER GOOD.
CHECK YOUR MORALS AND YOUR RESERVATIONS AT THE DOOR AND LET'S GET TO WORK.

DOMINION WORLD.
CONSIDER THIS JUSTICE.
BENEATH YOUR INCOMPETENT RULE, THE DOMINION FALTERED. IT GREW WEAK.
PATHETIC.
IT IS TIME FOR THE DOMINION TO BE REBORN--TO EVOLVE.
JUST AS I HAVE EVOLVED.
AT FIRST, I THOUGHT I WOULD SHARE THIS GIFT WITH MY PEOPLE. TOGETHER, WE WOULD BECOME A MASTER RACE.
HOW NAIVE I WAS.
YOUR MINDS ARE SMALL. YOU CANNOT SEE AS I DO. YOU ARE NOT WORTHY TO SHARE IN MY DIVINITY.
INSTEAD, YOU WILL WORSHIP ME.
ONE SMALL DEMONSTRATION OF MY POWER IS ALL IT WILL TAKE. SOMETHING YOU NEVER CAME CLOSE TO ACHIEVING.
THE EARTH WILL FALL BEFORE ME.
MYSELF... AND MY FIRST APOSTLE.

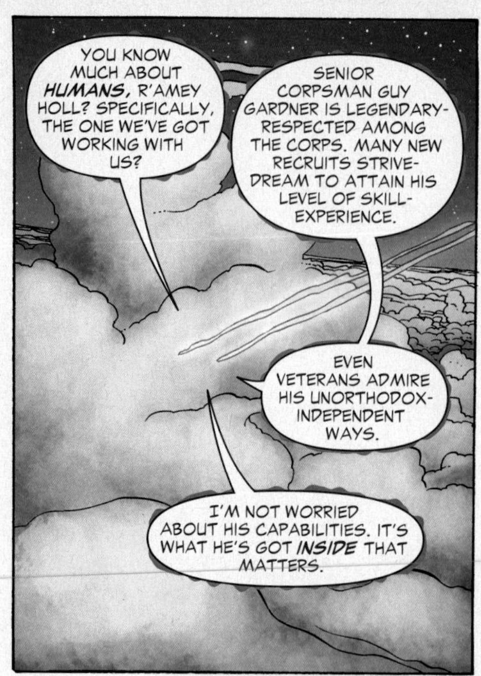

YOU KNOW MUCH ABOUT HUMANS, R'AMEY HOLL? SPECIFICALLY, THE ONE WE'VE GOT WORKING WITH US?
SENIOR CORPSMAN GUY GARDNER IS LEGENDARY-RESPECTED AMONG THE CORPS. MANY NEW RECRUITS STRIVE-DREAM TO ATTAIN HIS LEVEL OF SKILL-EXPERIENCE.
EVEN VETERANS ADMIRE HIS UNORTHODOX-INDEPENDENT WAYS.
I'M NOT WORRIED ABOUT HIS CAPABILITIES. IT'S WHAT HE'S GOT INSIDE THAT MATTERS.

HUMANS ARE A STRANGE BREED. THAT LIFETIME OF MORAL CONDITIONING IS ALMOST IMPOSSIBLE TO OVERCOME.
I'M AFRAID HE'S NOT HARDWIRED FOR THIS KIND OF WORK. THAT LEAVES ALL OF US AT GREAT RISK.
HE QUESTIONS-STRUGGLES WITH THIS ASSIGNMENT, BUT HIS WILLPOWER IS RARE-ASTONISHING.
I HAVE FAITH-BELIEF IN HIM.

THAT WHY YOU KISSED HIM?

HIS EMOTIONS-DOUBTS WERE BEGINNING TO OVERWHELM HIM.
I ACTED TO TEMPORARILY DISTRACT-REMOVE THOSE FEELINGS.

GOOD.

GOOD SOLDIER.

THE CLOCK IS TICKING. ENOUGH CHITCHAT.

TO KILL OR NOT TO KILL.

YOUR MIND SWINGS BACK AND FORTH, LANTERN GARDNER. I COULD LISTEN FOR *HOURS* AND NEVER GROW BORED.

MY STOMACH *RUMBLES,* THOUGH...

...AND I'VE GNAWED ON NOTHING BUT *BONES* FOR DAYS.

AGGHHH!
I AM A THOUSAND BLADES INSIDE YOUR HEAD, HUMAN.
DISSECTING YOUR THOUGHTS.
DEVOURING YOUR MEMORIES.
focus... Gardner...
...willpower...
...out of... my...
URK!
KRAK

YOUR THOUGHTS ARE GAMEY, HUMAN.
I WONDER, WILL YOUR FLESH BE MORE TENDER?
get...
...get...
...get...
OFF!

WHAMMM

...DAMN KHUND...

...SICK FREAK...
MY BRAIN FEELS LIKE...
...LIKE A BLACK HOLE.
A HUMAN.
IN THE HEART OF THE DOMINION.
WHAT A MAGNIFICENT SURPRISE.
SHOW YOU WHAT I DO...
...TO FREAKS LIKE YOU...

ORIGINALLY, THERE WAS A ROGUE AMONG THE GUARDIANS. HE RECRUITED A HANDFUL OF US FROM THE CORPS TO PURSUE HIS OWN AGENDA.
I DIDN'T KNOW ANY OF THIS UNTIL LATER ON, AND BY THEN, I ALREADY BELIEVED IN HIS CAUSE.
HAVING A SOUL IS OVERRATED, ANYWAY. ALL IT DOES IS GET IN THE WAY OF DOING GOOD.
THERE ARE PLACES IN THE UNIVERSE THAT ARE JUST TOO DARK FOR THE LIGHT OF THE CORPS TO SHINE, R'AMEY HOLL.
THOSE ARE THE SHADOWS WE LIVED IN.
UNTIL...
RECOGNIZE THIS FACE?
HAL JORDAN. THE ONCE-PRESENT GREATEST OF ALL GREEN LANTERNS.
YEAH, HE'S SPECIAL ALL RIGHT.
WHEN JORDAN TOOK DOWN THE CORPS, MY MEN WERE STRANDED UNDER DEEP COVER, POWERLESS, IN THE WORST PITS OF THE UNIVERSE.
"DIE ALONE," THAT WAS OUR MOTTO. BUT NOT LIKE THAT. MY BOYS DESERVED BETTER.
I'M LOOKING FORWARD TO MEETING HAL JORDAN SOME-DAY.

I WAS ONE OF THE FEW THAT SURVIVED. I WENT UNDER-GROUND SOMEWHERE SAFE, OUT OF THE WAY.
I KNEW IT WAS ONLY A MATTER OF TIME. THERE'S STILL WORK TO BE DONE, THERE ALWAYS WILL BE. IN SPITE OF EVERYTHING, I STILL BELIEVE THIS IS THE WAY TO DO IT.
NOW PAY ATTENTION. LET ME SHOW YOU A LITTLE TRICK.
YOU'VE USED YOUR RING BEFORE TO SCAN FOR LIFE. SAME PRINCIPLE, DIFFERENT OBJECTIVE. IN THIS CASE, WE'RE LOOKING FOR A UNIQUE RADIOACTIVE SIGNATURE.
THOSE LITTLE GREEN TRINKETS ARE A LITTLE...OBVIOUS...SO IN THE CORPSE EVERYTHING STAYS HIDDEN INSIDE, INCONSPICUOUS.
WE'RE LIVING RINGS FOR AS LONG AS OUR CHARGE LASTS.
FOCUS YOUR WILL OUTWARD. KEEP YOUR THOUGHTS FAST AND TIGHT. VISUALIZE YOUR GOAL.
IT'S MUCH MORE VERSATILE THAN THOSE CLUNKY RINGS.
THERE IT IS.

UNGHH!
ON... YOUR...FEET... GARDNER...
...KICK... THIS BUM'S... ASS...
RISE, MY APOSTLE. YOUR EDUCATION WILL NOW BEGIN.
THERE IS A MYSTERY HERE.
YOU ARE FAR FROM HOME, HUMAN, SWIMMING IN DEADLY WATERS.
TELL ME WHY.
PTOO!
WATCH CLOSELY, MY APOSTLE.
LET ME TEACH YOU ABOUT PAIN.

NOOO!
...WORRY-THINK TOO MUCH...
...ARTIFACT IS A SPACE ROCK...
...IS ABOUT DUTY. NOW LET'S GET TO WORK...
AARRH!

I'M SHUTTING DOWN YOUR HIGHER FUNCTIONS, EARTHLING. ALL EXCEPT FOR ONE...
YOUR PAIN RECEPTORS WILL CONTINUE TO FUNCTION AS YOUR BODY SLOWLY WITHERS AWAY.
SUFFER AND DIE THE WAY ALL HUMANS SHOULD.

A GUARDIAN IS BEHIND HIS PRESENCE. HE MOVES TO THWART ME.
LET US SPELL HIM A MESSAGE WITH THE CORPSES OF HIS PUPPETS.
COME. THIS LANTERN'S ALLIES AWAIT.
FUMP

NOT MUCH TO LOOK AT, IS IT? POWER LEVELS ARE STRATOSPHERIC THOUGH. WHATEVER THIS THING IS, IT'S HOT.
OUR DISCS WILL PROTECT US FROM THE RADIATION, AT LEAST FOR A BIT. YOU GOT ANY IDEAS ON HOW TO SAFELY DESTROY THIS THING, THINK FAST. NOW'S NOT THE TIME TO BE SHY.
THE FIRST-SAFEST THOUGHT IS TO REMOVE-DEPOSIT IT IN--
SKOOOM
DURLAN!
TIME TO DIE... JUST LIKE YOUR LITTLE HUMAN FRIEND!
SENIOR CORPSMAN GARDNER?!?
CAN'T WORRY ABOUT HIM NOW. GET RID OF THAT ASTEROID!
I'LL TAKE CARE OF THIS KHUND PIECE OF--
GAAHH!
THE WALLS AROUND YOUR MIND ARE THIN, DURLAN.
PITY. I HAD HOPED THIS WOULD BE A CHALLENGE.
e...ev...EVER...
EVER HEAR OF A THANAGARIAN HAWK-SLUG? UGLY, BUT ITS BRAIN IS A THING OF BEAUTY.
OVER THE MILLENNIA, IT'S EVOLVED A NATURAL DEFENSE AGAINST TELEPATHIC ASSAULTS.
AAR!
GUESS WHAT I'VE JUST MORPHED MY BRAIN INTO, KHUND?
KRAK

THE ORB-SUN.
MUST DELIVER-REACH THE ORB-SUN--
I SAW YOU IN THE HUMAN'S MIND BEFORE I KILLED HIM.
YOU HAVE SOMETHING THAT BELONGS TO ME...GREEN LANTERN.
DIE!
HEH.

STRUGGLE, BY ALL MEANS. EVEN A GOD NEEDS TO LAUGH.
IN THE MEANTIME, YOUR LITTLE BAND OF ROGUES HAS PIQUED MY CURIOSITY. YOU WORK FOR THE GUARDIANS YET YOU ARE NOT TRULY GREEN LANTERNS.
THERE IT IS.
I WONDER... WHERE DOES YOUR POWER COME FROM IF YOU HAVE NO RING?
AH, YES...
SPLOOORTCH
FASCINATING.
EVERYTHING A LANTERN RING CAN DO AND NOW...
SHLURP
...IT BELONGS TO ME.

HAHA HAHAHA HA!
THE POWER!
EVEN DARKSEID WOULD NOW TREMBLE IN MY SHADOW!
THE DURLAN'S INTESTINES WERE SURPRISINGLY TENDER.
THEY MADE A FINE MEAL, MASTER.
I HAVE BECOME SOMETHING THE UNIVERSE HAS NEVER KNOWN, KHUND. KNEEL BEFORE ME, PLEDGE YOUR FEALTY.
I AM YOUR HUMBLE APOSTLE, MY LORD: A WEAPON IN YOUR FIST.
SHOW ME THE WAY AND IT WILL BE DONE.
EARTH.

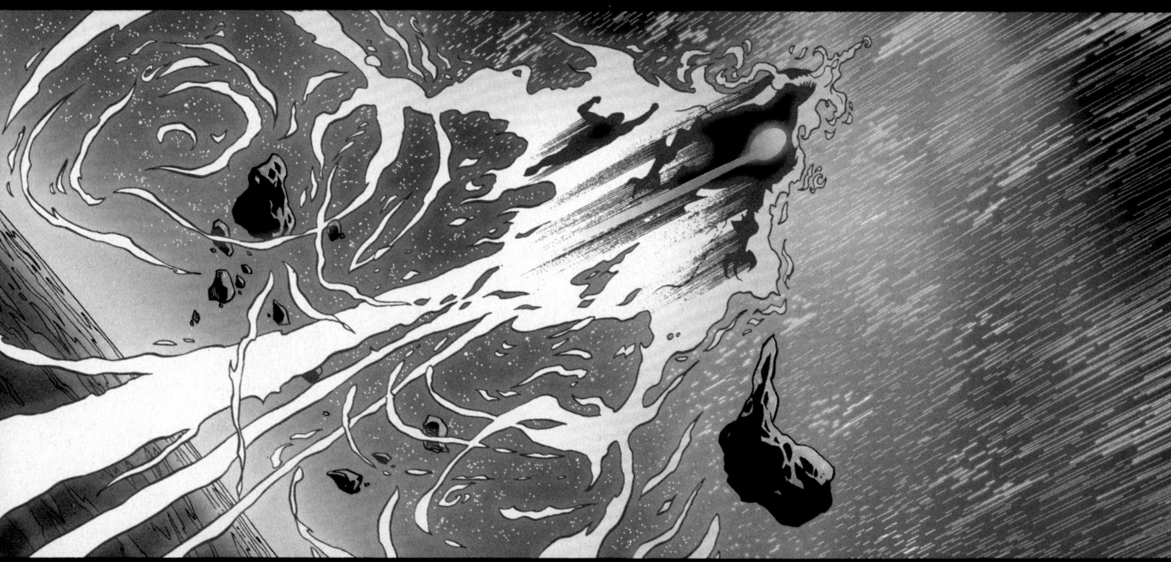

GREEN LANTERN CORPS #9
Cover by Patrick Gleason, Wayne Faucher and Moose Baumann

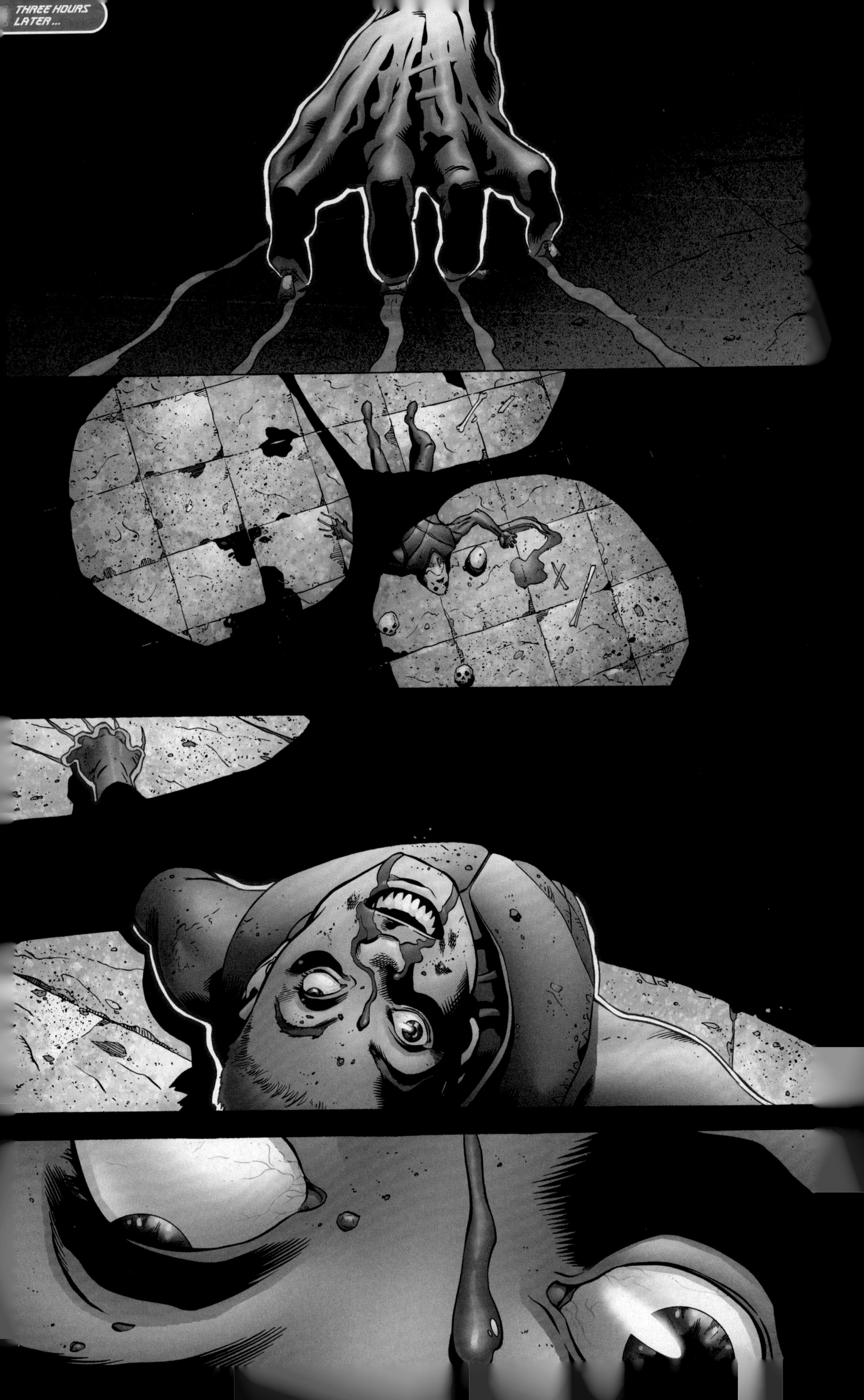
THREE HOURS LATER...

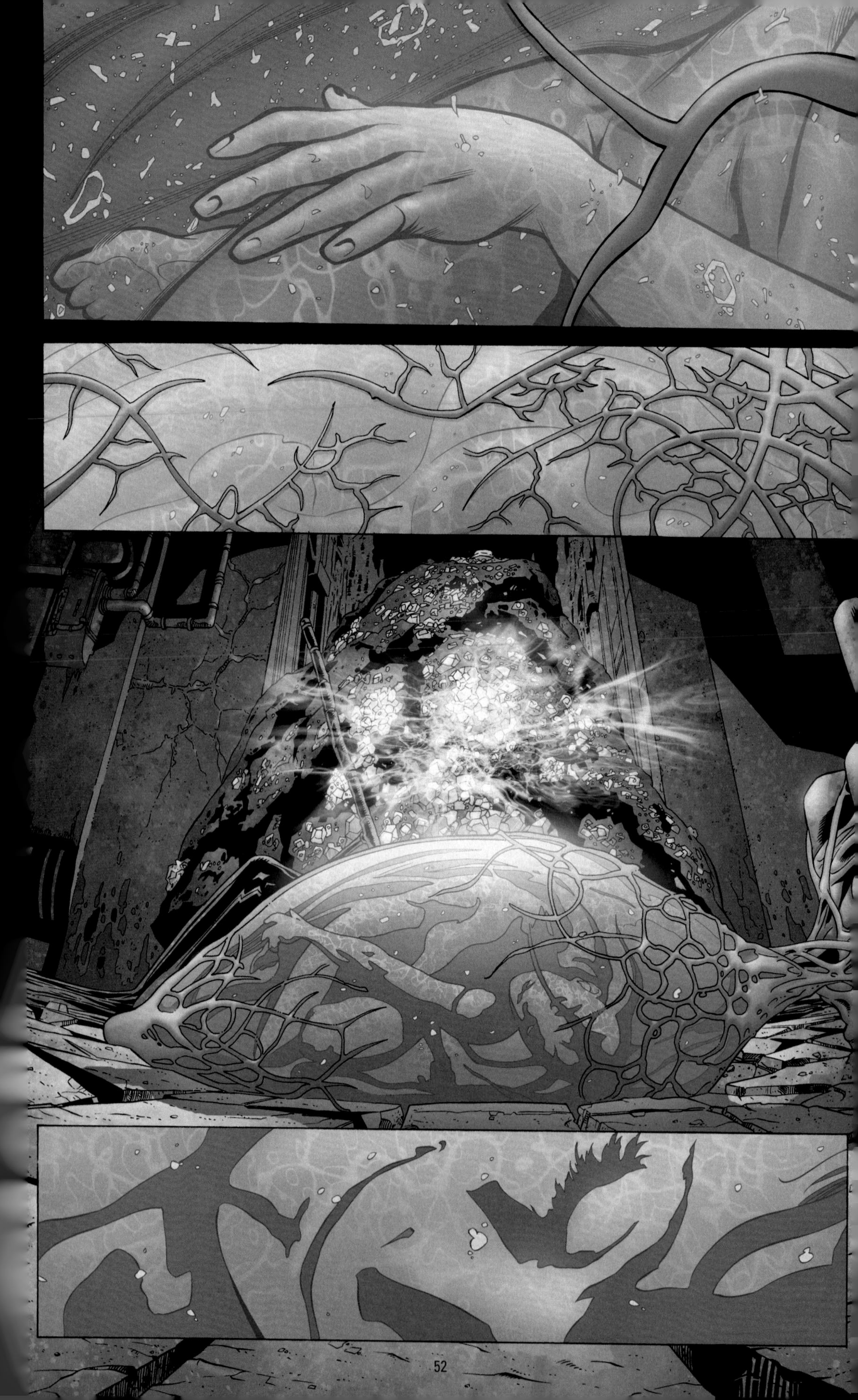

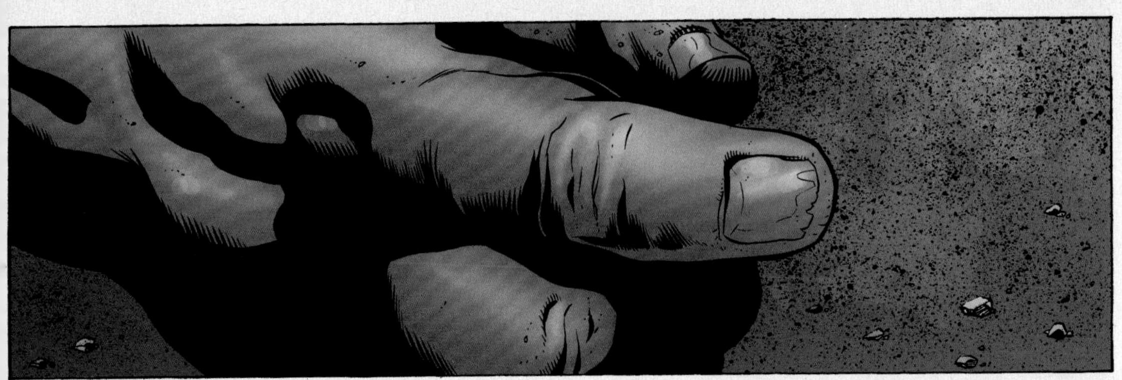

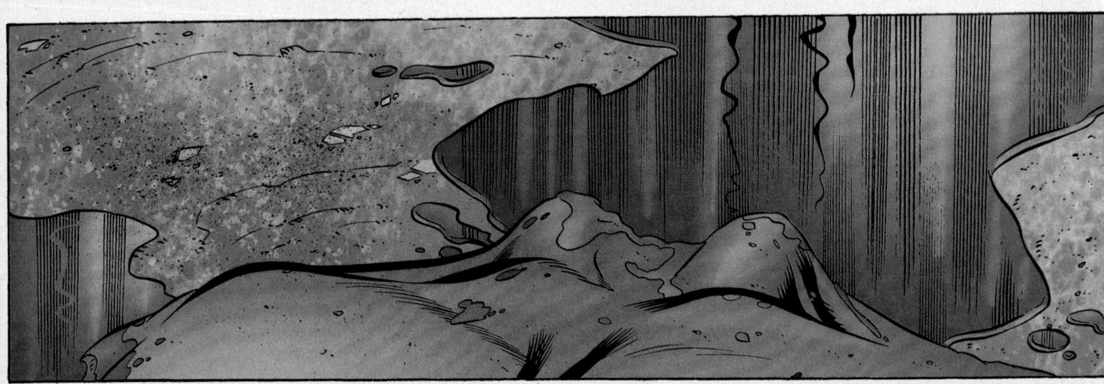

SIMULTANEOUSLY...
THE DARK SIDE OF GREEN
CONCLUSION
KEITH CHAMPAGNE writer PATRICK GLEASON penciller
PRENTIS ROLLINS & RAY SNYDER inkers MOOSE BAUMANN colorist PHIL BALSMAN letterer

WHERE
ARE
THEY?!

THIS HAS ALL GONE WRONG!
HOW MANY ROTATIONS DID I STUDY THE DOMINION'S INTELLIGENCE FROM THE GREAT INVASION?
HOW MANY EVENINGS DID I SPEND STRATEGIZING THE PERFECT PLAN OF ATTACK?
IT WAS ALL TO BEGIN HERE, IN THIS FROZEN WASTELAND, HOME OF ONE OF THEIR PATHETIC LITTLE JUSTICE TEAMS.
THE GROWING SENSE OF UNEASE WHEN COMMUNICATION WAS SUDDENLY LOST--RIPPLES OF PANIC SPREADING WITH WORD OF THEIR DEATHS.

ALL TO HERALD THE UNSTOPPABLE RETURN OF THE DOMINION!

I HAVE DREAMT OF THIS MOMENT, MY DISCIPLE, AND MY DREAM HAS GONE ASTRAY.

AWAY.
I MUST NOW IMPROVISE.

UURF!

IT MATTERS NOT.
THE SUPERMAN IS KNOWN TO INHABIT THE EARTH CITY CALLED METROPOLIS.
HIS DEATH WILL BETTER SERVE TO ANNOUNCE MY ARRIVAL.
COME, URUK. LET US DROWN THIS PLANET IN BLOOD AND--
THIS WORLD BELONGS TO DARKSEID.
YOUR PRESENCE HERE DISRUPTS MY CAREFUL MACHINATIONS, FOOL.

DOMINION WORLD
KRRKKK
SENIOR CORPSMAN GARDNER... I FEEL-HEAR YOU?
THE SENSATION IS... BIZARRE-WONDERFUL.
NO!
YOUR LIFE-SOUL IS ALMOST DWINDLED-GONE.
THIS MUST NOT BE ALLOWED TO PASS-OCCUR!

SENIOR CORPSMAN GARDNER!
I CAN...VISUAL SENSE... THE DAMAGE IN YOUR SELF-MIND.
IT IS MORTAL-SEVERE.
YOUR NEURAL-THOUGHT PATHS HAVE BEEN ERASED-EXTINGUISHED.
CLING TO MY VOICE-THOUGHTS, SENIOR CORPSMAN.
WHEN I FIRST LEARNED I WAS PARTNERED-ASSIGNED WITH THE LEGENDARY-RESPECTED SENIOR CORPSMAN GARDNER FOR MY FIRST TASK-MISSION...
...I COULD BARELY CONTAIN-CONCEAL MY EXCITEMENT-FLUSH. I FELT LIKE A CHILD-STUDENT IN THE THROES OF FIRST PASSION-LOVE.
NO MATTER WHAT I HAVE BECOME-EVOLVED, WHEN I LOOK IN YOUR EYES...
...MY HEART WILL NOT LET YOU PASS-EXPIRE.

phuuu--
SENIOR CORPSMAN GARDNER, YOU ARE...FUNCTIONAL-RESTORED?
NORMALLY, I'D BE HACKED OFF IF A BROAD TOOK ADVANTAGE OF ME WHILE I WAS DOWN.
ACTUALLY, THAT'S A *LIE.*
DON'T KNOW WHAT YOU DID, BUT MY *BRAIN* FEELS SPIT-POLISHED.
DIG THE NEW LOOK, BY THE WAY. NAKED SUITS YOU, R'AMEY.
LAST THING I REMEMBER, AN UGLY YELLOW MOTHER KICKED MY ASS AND LEFT ME TO ROT.
LOOKS LIKE I MISSED OUT ON SOME ACTION.
WE'D BETTER GET MOVING. CATCH ME UP ON THE WAY.
OH...AND R'AMEY?
I GOT A LITTLE *TINGLE* THE FIRST TIME I SAW YOU, TOO.
LET'S GO SAVE THE UNIVERSE AND THEN WE'LL

IT IS ELUSIVE-DIFFICULT, BUT IF I STRETCH-PROJECT MY THOUGHTS, I CAN SENSE-FEEL THE DOMINATOR'S MIND.
HE IS ON EARTH.
DAGGLE IS WITH HIM, SUBTERFUGE-DISGUISED.
YOU PICKED UP ALL KINDS OF PARTY TRICKS WHILE I WAS NAPPING, DIDN'T YOU? MAYBE I SHOULD TAKE A BATH WITH THAT CHUNK OF ROCK MYSELF.
ON SECOND THOUGHT, I'M PERFECT AS IS. GOTTA HAND IT TO THE DURLAN, THOUGH, HE'S GOT A PAIR OF BRASS ONES.
PROBLEM IS, EVEN WITH A NORMAL RING AT FULL BLAST, IT'S STILL GONNA TAKE US AT LEAST HALF A DAY TO GET BACK TO EARTH.
THIS LITTLE BLACK DISC IN MY GUT PROBABLY CAN'T DO MUCH BETTER.
SENIOR CORPSMAN GARDNER?
I HAVE AN IDEA-SUGGESTION.
THE BLACK HOLE EXPRESS, EH?
YOU'RE JUST FULL OF NEW TRICKS, AREN'T YOU?
ANYTHING ELSE I SHOULD KNOW ABOUT--ASIDE FROM PERFECT TIMING?
COME-FOLLOW, SENIOR CORPSMAN.
TIME TO TANGO.

EARTH.
IT IS VERY SIMPLE, INSECT. LEAVE THIS SYSTEM OR SUFFER MY WRATH.
DARKSEID DOES NOT ASK.
I AM NOT ONE OF YOUR LOWLY HUNGER DOGS, DARKSEID. I AM THE DOMINATOR.
I WILL NOT BE BARKED AT.

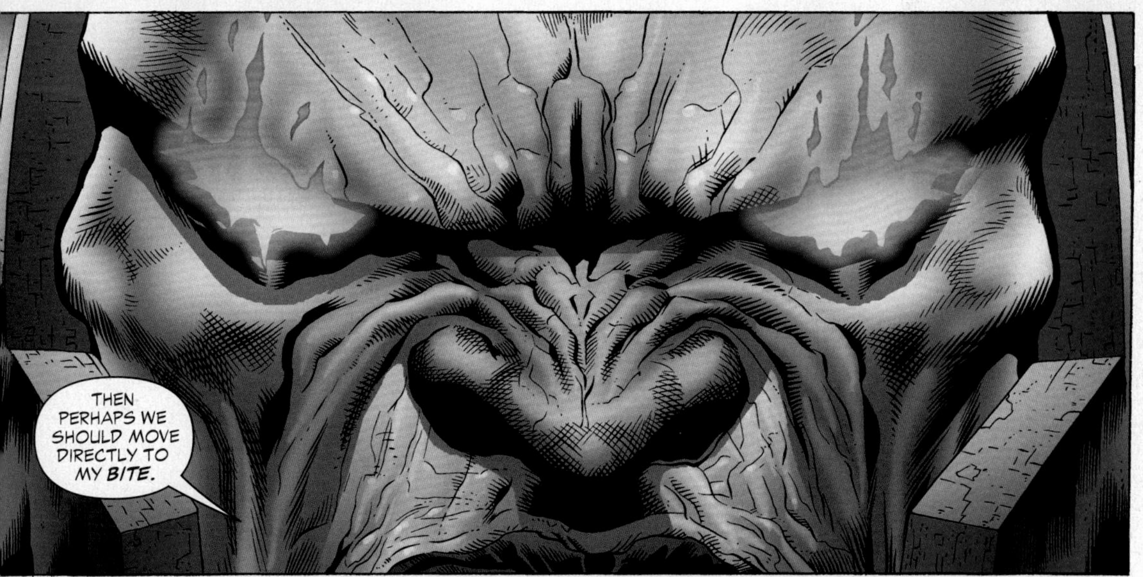
THEN PERHAPS WE SHOULD MOVE DIRECTLY TO MY BITE.

GREAT ARKSEID--HOLD! MY DISCIPLE AND DIDN'T INTEND TO DISRUPT YOUR PLANS.
WE ONLY SEEK TO--

WAIT.
WHERE IS MY DISCIPLE?
FOR THAT MATTER, WHY WAS THERE NO BOOM TO HERALD YOUR ARRIVAL?
...DAMNATION...

YOUR KHUNDISH LAPDOG, URUK, FORGOT HE COULDN'T SURVIVE WITHOUT HIS HEAD, DOMINATOR.
I HAD TO REMIND HIM.
NOW IT'S YOUR TURN.
YOU KILLED MY DISCIPLE?
TZZZAK
TZZZAK
TZZAK
ARRGH!

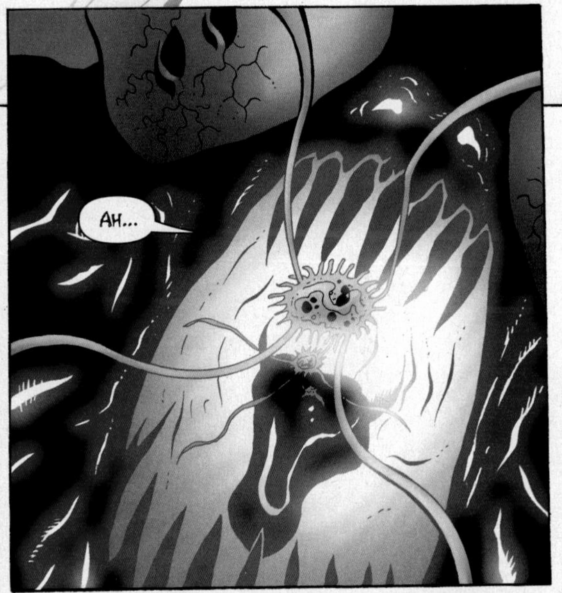
AH...

PATHETIC... ALTHOUGH STRANGELY APPROPRIATE.
FOR WHAT ARE YOU IF NOT A BACTERIUM IN THE FACE OF WHAT I HAVE BECOME?

TIME TO MEET YOUR END, DURLAN.

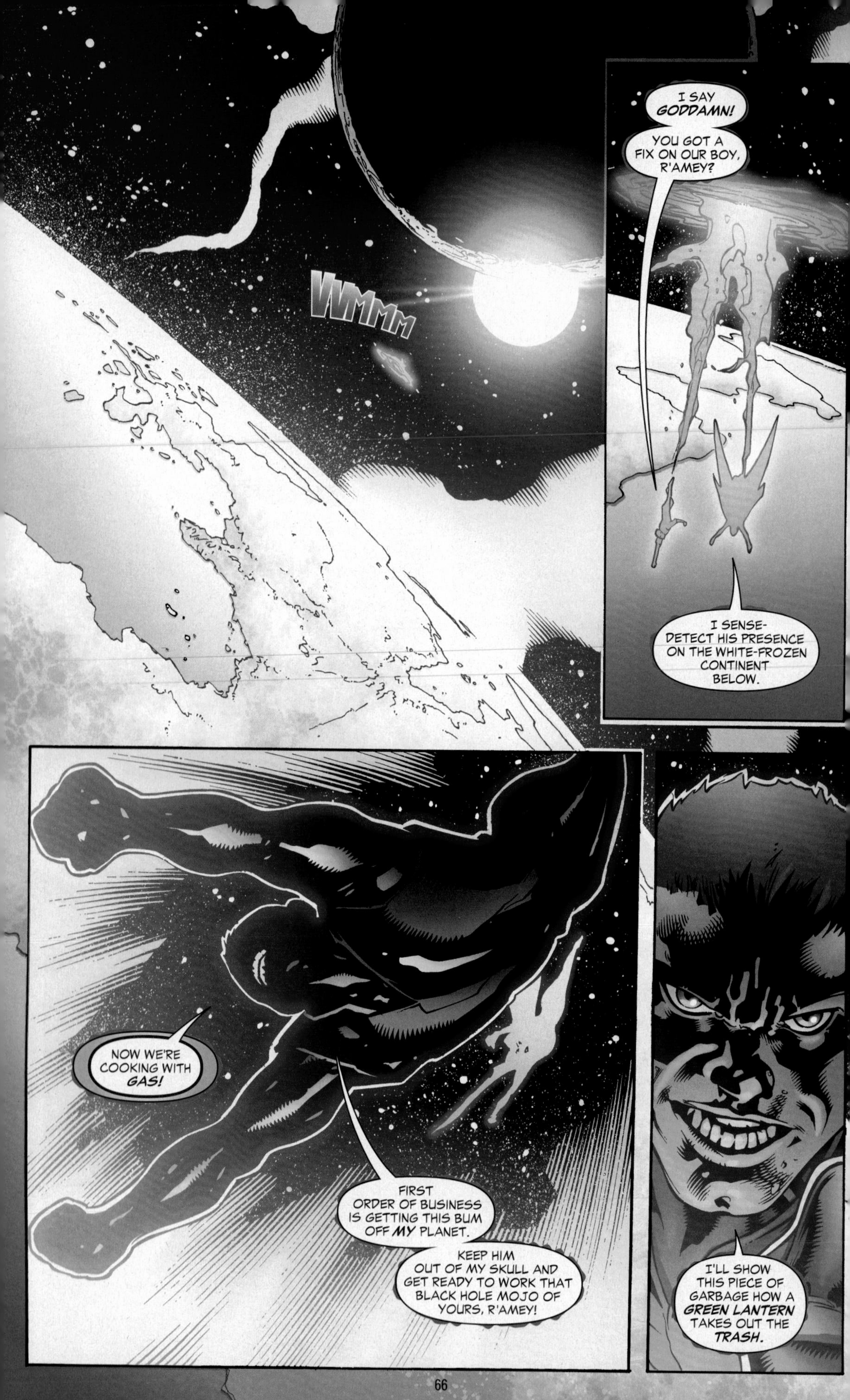
VVMMM
I SAY GODDAMN!
YOU GOT A FIX ON OUR BOY, R'AMEY?
I SENSE-DETECT HIS PRESENCE ON THE WHITE-FROZEN CONTINENT BELOW.
NOW WE'RE COOKING WITH GAS!
FIRST ORDER OF BUSINESS IS GETTING THIS BUM OFF MY PLANET.
KEEP HIM OUT OF MY SKULL AND GET READY TO WORK THAT BLACK HOLE MOJO OF YOURS, R'AMEY!
I'LL SHOW THIS PIECE OF GARBAGE HOW A GREEN LANTERN TAKES OUT THE TRASH.

CAN YOU FEEL THAT, DURLAN?
IT'S THE WEIGHT OF THE UNIVERSE BEARING DOWN ON YOUR SHOULDERS.
CAN YOU STAND UP TO THE PRESSURE?
NOW!
HNN?
WHAMMM

WMMM
C'MERE UGLY...
...GOT SOMETHING FOR YOU...
RAAAA--
--AAAAAAAGH!
PROBLEM, DOMINATOR? CAN'T HANDLE THE PRESSURE?
BECAUSE WE'RE JUST GETTING WARMED UP.
DAGGLE!
TZZAK
TZZAK

STRAIGHT UP.
CLASS IS NOW IN SESSION.
SKOOOM
KZZAK
AIIIE!
FWAM
NO...
...PLEASE...
...I'M... JUST A SCIENTIST THAT...
ASK ME IF I CARE, LOSER.
AND THAT'S THE NAME OF THAT TUNE.
NNN...
LET'S WRAP HIM UP AND GET HIM BACK TO OA. LET THE GUARDIANS DECIDE WHAT TO DO WITH HIM.
NO.
THE TASK-MISSION IS NOT COMPLETE.

I DON'T LIKE WHERE YOU'RE GOING WITH--
WHOOF!
VVMMM
VVMMM
SHRRRPP
NOW WE ARE FINISHED- COMPLETE.

END OF THE LINE, GARDNER. ALL THE MOPPING UP IS DONE. THIS IS WHERE WE FORGET WE EVER KNEW EACH OTHER.
THAT A FACT? BECAUSE I'M DONE FOLLOWING YOUR ORDERS, DAGGLE
A FACT IT IS...WHETHER YOU LIKE IT OR NOT.
YOU'RE A WASHOUT, GARDNER. THERE'S NO PLACE FOR YOU IN THE CORPSE.
EARTHLINGS NEVER MAKE THE CUT. YOU JUST DON'T HAVE WHAT IT TAKES.
DON'T ASK WHERE I KEPT IT HIDDEN.
TAKE A COUPLE OF DAYS OFF UNTIL YOUR BLACK CHARGE RUNS DRY.
SUIT BACK UP. GO DO SOME GOOD.
DON'T WORRY. WE'LL BE OUT HERE DOING THE HEAVY LIFTING.
TRUTH IS, I AIN'T NEVER BEEN SO PROUD OF FAILING IN MY ENTIRE LIFE.
KILLING SOMEONE, THAT'S THE EASY WAY OUT. MAKING THE SCUM OF THE UNIVERSE FACE THE MUSIC...THAT'S MORE MY STYLE.
WHATEVER HELPS YOU SLEEP.
BY THE WAY, YOUR GIRLFRIEND IS WAITING UP AHEAD.
SWEET KID. SHE DIDN'T WANT TO LEAVE WITHOUT SAYING GOODBYE.

YOU MIGHT AS WELL SAVE YOUR BREATH. YOU MADE YOUR CHOICE, AND I MADE MINE. I'M NOT WASTING TIME THINKING ABOUT WHAT MIGHT HAVE BEEN.
IT'S A DAMN SHAME, THOUGH, R'AMEY.
FOR A LITTLE WHILE THERE, IT FELT LIKE WE HAD SOMETHING... REAL... going on, I--
WHUMP
SACRIFICE IS NEVER EASY, R'AMEY. THAT'S WHY IT'S CALLED SACRIFICE.
HE CAN'T BE ALLOWED TO REMEMBER. THERE'S NO ROOM FOR ERROR.
HE WILL RECALL-REMEMBER NOTHING EXCEPT FAILING TO LOCATE VON DAGGLE ON CORONA SEVEN. TRAGICALLY, HIS PARTNER WAS LOST IN A STORM-AVALANCHE.
SINCE THEN, SENIOR CORPSMAN GARDNER HAS SPENT SEVERAL DAYS ALONE-WANDERING IN SPACE WITH HIS GUILT-THOUGHTS BEFORE RETURNING TO OA.
GOOD SOLDIER.
LET'S GET BACK TO THE DOMINION BEFORE THAT CHUNK OF ROCK FALLS INTO THE WRONG HANDS. THEN WE HEAD BACK TO CORONA SEVEN AND WAIT.
NOW THAT WE'RE BACK IN BUSINESS, IT WON'T BE LONG BEFORE WE'RE CONTACTED AGAIN.

FIFTEEN MINUTES EARLIER...

HOW STRANGE.

I'VE NEVER...

I'VE NEVER SEEN ANYTHING QUITE LIKE IT. WHAT SORT OF VALUE COULD I ASSIGN TO--

FAASH

ARRGH!

GREEN LANTERN CORPS #10
Cover by Patrick Gleason, Rodney Ramos and Moose Baumann

OA.
THE MATTER IS CLOSED, LANTERN GARDNER. YOUR SHORE LEAVE ON RESTORIA WAS INDEED CUT SHORT--
--BUT THAT WAS DUE TO YOUR OWN NEGLIGENCE IN LOSING YOUR POWER RING.
IF NOT FOR MY INTERVENTION, YOU MIGHT HAVE LOST YOUR LIFE, TOO.
SHORE LEAVE REVOKED FOR A FURTHER YEAR.
FRIENDS IN NEED
DAVE GIBBONS ▪ WRITER DAVE GIBBONS & PATRICK GLEASON ▪ PENCILLERS
DAVE GIBBONS & CHRISTIAN ALAMY ▪ INKERS
MOOSE BAUMANN ▪ COLORIST PHIL BALSMAN ▪ LETTERER

NOW, PLEASE, LEAVE ME. I HAVE MUCH TO DO.
LIKE I DON'T?
I NEVER GET A BREAK! HELPIN' A NEWBIE HERE, BAILIN' OUT SOME JACKASS LANTERN WHO'S GOT HIS SPANDEX IN A BUNCH THERE...
...WE ALL NEED TIME OUT, SALAAK. EVEN YOU HUNG OUT ON RESTORIA AFTER ME, UP TO STUFF I DON'T EVEN WANT TA SEE IN MY HEAD.
AN' KILOWOG'S BUCKLED UP AS TIGHT AS A DRUM. WHEN DID HE LAST KICK BACK?
TELL YA ONE THING, I DON'T WANNA BE AROUND WHEN THAT POOZER'S BELT BREAKS!
I'M SURE TRAINING OFFICER KILOWOG WOULD APPRECIATE YOUR CONCERN--BUT HE IS, AS YOU EARTHMEN SAY, A BIG BOY NOW.
IF ONLY YOU SHOWED THE SAME MATURITY.
SEE YOU ON THE BEACH LATER, EH?
BAH.
NOW, ABOUT GRADUATION DAY...

NOW, GRADUATION DAY FOR THE TRAINEES IS NEAR, AND I HAVE MUCH TO DISCUSS WITH MY SENIOR LANTERNS.
TO YOUR ASSIGNMENT, GARDNER.
NOW.
YOU FINAGLE ANY SHORE LEAVE YET, GARDNER?
SHOULDN'T YOU BE IN CLUSTRAL, POOZER?
YEAH, YEAH. ON MY WAY.
PICKLEHEAD.

SECTOR 1417.
KORUGAR.
S'MINE. I CAUGHT IT.
YOU MIGHTA CAUGHT IT, BUT I SAW IT AND WOUNDED IT.
I CAUGHT IT, I KILLED IT.
I'M GONNA EAT IT.
NO.
YOU SHARE IT!
I KILLED IT.
I KILL YOU, TOO.
SHUNK
AGGHHH!
NO!

STOP!
A LANTERN! RUN, BROTHERS. THE GREEN EVIL IS AMONG US!
SOME OF US CAN'T RUN, BROTHER.
DON'T BE AFRAID. LET ME HELP...
BLOOD PRESSURE FALLING. PULSE CRITICAL. BLOOD LOSS UNSUSTAINABLE.
I-I'm dying...
BUT YOU'RE NOT DEAD YET. NOT IF I CAN HELP IT.
WHAT'S SHE DOIN'?
RING. INHIBIT THE PAIN REFLEX IN HIS FRONTAL LOBES.
MONITOR VITAL SIGNS. STIMULATE CARDIAC FUNCTION.

I THINK SHE'S MENDIN' HIM WITH THAT RING O' HERS.
I HEARD THE LANTERN RINGS ONLY KILLED AND CORRUPTED.
THERE.
YOU BETTER TAKE IT EASY FOR A WHILE.
TH-THANK YOU.
YOU'RE WELCOME.
I HAVE TO GO NOW.
NO.
WAIT.
PLEASE...
PLEASE... HEAL US, TOO.

SECTOR 2684.
CLUSTRAL.
EXITING TRANSLUMINAL.
SO WHAT HAPPENED HERE-- AND WHERE ARE THE LAYABOUTS WHO OUGHTTA BE HANDLIN' IT?
ANOMALOUS MATTER DISCHARGE FROM THE WHITE DWARF STAR AT THE CENTER OF THE SYSTEM DISRUPTED THE ORBITING ENVIRONMENT.
STRUCTURE REQUIRES URGENT STABILIZATION AND REPAIR BEFORE LOCALIZED ATMOSPHERE IS COMPROMISED.
LANTERNS QUOND AND TANAKATA Z ON SCENE. HOMING ON THEIR RING-BEACONS.
TAKE ME TO 'EM.

HEY, TANAKATA Z. HEADS UP. CAVALRY'S HERE.
GLORY-HUNTING MAN-APE, MORE LIKE.
HOW ARE THINGS HANGIN' HERE?
EVERYTHING IS UNDER CONTROL, LANTERN GARDNER. YOUR ASSISTANCE IS REDUNDANT.
THAT SO?
WELL, OA THINKS YOU GOLDBRICKS HAVE BEEN DRAGGIN' YOUR ASSES AND WANTS ME TO GET THIS SEWN UP, PRONTO.
IT'S A COMPLEX ASTROPHYSICAL TASK-- AND LAST WE HEARD YOU HAD TROUBLE JUST LYIN' ON A SUNBED THESE DAYS.
HAH, HAH. GOOD ONE, TANAK.
COUPLE O' JOKERS, EH? YOU GOT SOMETHIN' TO ADD, WISEGUY?
HEY, J-JUST A LITTLE HUMOR TO LIGHTEN THE DAY.
WELL, I AIN'T SMILIN'. AND WHEN I AIN'T SMILIN', TROUBLE'S COMIN'.
WANT SOME TROUBLE?
N-NO, HONOR LANTERN GARDNER.

GOOD.
YOU RUBES NEED SOME METHOD ON THIS.
QUOND, YOU CHECK AND REPAIR THE STRANDS AROUND THE EDGE OF THE TEAR.
YOUR BIG-MOUTH BUDDY SECURES THE PLANETOIDS AND CROSS-ATTACHES THEM.

I'LL SWEEP FOR LOOSE PLANETOIDS AND STRAY NATIVES, BRING 'EM IN FOR YOU TO REATTACH.
YOU GOT THAT, TOO, DRAGON BOY?
YES, SIR.

WE DO THE GRUNT WORK, HE GETS THE CREDIT.
AH, HE'S OKAY. LET'S JUST GET THIS DUSTED.

YOU SCARED OF HIM, QUOND?
HONOR GUARD OR NO HONOR GUARD, I WOULDN'T LET HIM TALK TO ME LIKE YOU JUST DID.

I'M NOT SCARED OF ANYTHING, TANAK. I JUST WANNA DO THE JOB AND GET OUTTA HERE.
RIIIGHT.

SECTOR 2261.
MOGO.
REALLY, I FEEL FINE NOW. THE HORMONE STORM IS OVER. THE URGE TO MATE IS GONE.
MEBBE. BUT THE WAY SHE CHEATED ON YOU-- ANY WARM-BLOODED MALE'S GOTTA BE CARRYIN' A LOAD OF ANGER.
THING IS, BUDDY, I AIN'T WARM-BLOODED.
I'M A REPTILE.
ANYWAY, WARM OR COLD, MOGO'LL HELP YOU.
HELPED ME WITH ALL THE ANGER I WAS HOLDING.

QALYRA COULDN'T HELP HERSELF. I'D HAVE DONE THE SAME, IF SHE'D GONE OFF SOMEPLACE.
WE'RE HERE ALREADY, SO JUST TALK TO MOGO, OK?

BEFORE YOU MAKE ME ANGRY AGAIN.

WHO--?

LANTERN 2828? ER, GREEN MAN? THAT YOUR NAME?
NAME? WE HAVE NO NEED OF NAMES.
HERE AS ON UXOR, ALL ARE ONE. JOIN US, BROTHER ISAMOT.
WE CAME HERE TROUBLED, LIKE YOU.
BUT NOW THINGS ARE SO CLEAR.
JOIN US.
ER. Y'KNOW WHAT...
I REALLY DON'T KNOW WHY I'M HERE.
VATH-- MY PARTNER-- MADE ME COME. BUT, HEY...
I GUESS I DON'T NEED MOGO'S HELP AS MUCH AS SOME.
SHAME TO WASTE THE BIG GUY'S TIME.
SEE YOU ON OA SOMETIME, GREENIE.

KORUGAR.
IT'S A LANTERN. HEARD SHE GOT THROWN OUTTA HER HOSPITAL JOB. NOW SHE'S FIXIN' US LOWDOWNS. OUR GAIN, HUH?
YEAH. GAIN IT IS.
FINDIN' HER HERE'S CERTAINLY GONNA DO ME GOOD.
YOU--YOU'LL HAVE TO BE THE LAST ONE FOR NOW.
MY CONCENTRATION IS FADING.
BUT, DOCTOR--WHAT ABOUT ME? THE PAIN...
I'M SORRY.
I'LL SEE YOU ONCE I'VE HAD SOME REST.
I NEED TO--
AAAAHH!
WHAT?
THOOOOOM

OUR INFORMANT WAS TELLING THE TRUTH.
WE HAVE EXPOSED NATU'S SEDITION.

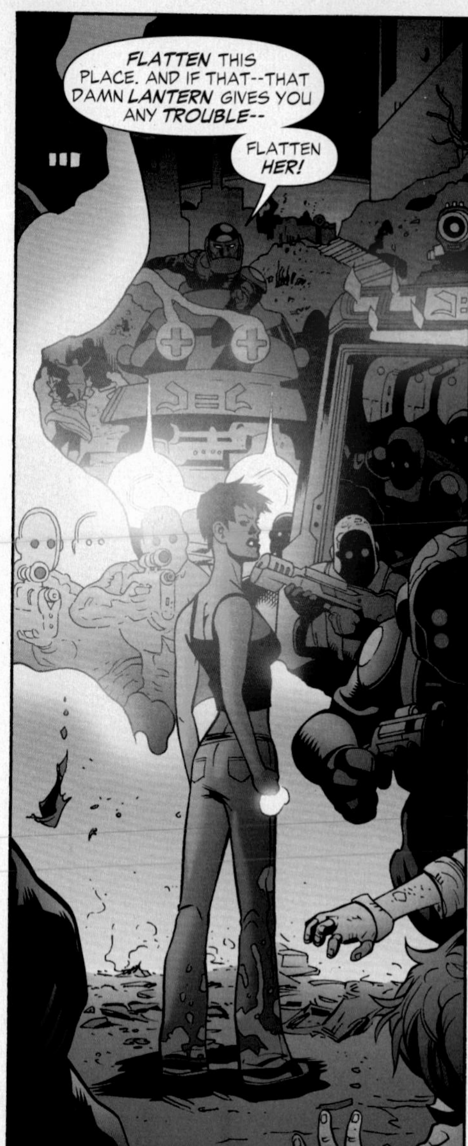
FLATTEN THIS PLACE. AND IF THAT--THAT DAMN LANTERN GIVES YOU ANY TROUBLE--
FLATTEN HER!

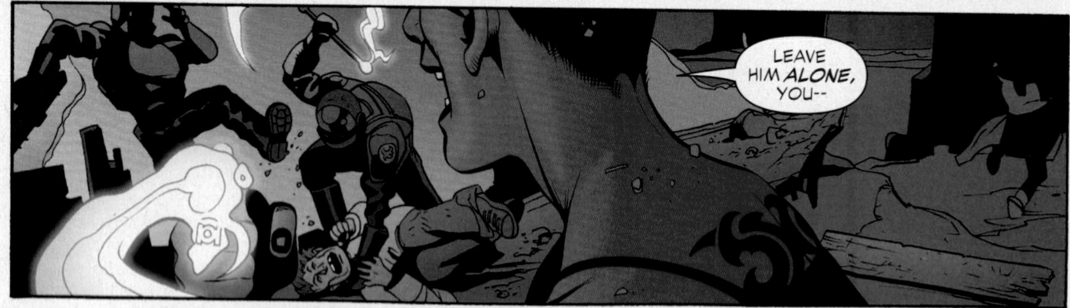
LEAVE HIM ALONE, YOU--

AAAAHH!
AAAAHH!

THAT'S IT. SHE ASSAULTED TWO OF OUR OWN.
BRING HER DOWN. WHATEVER IT TAKES!
TRAITORS AND CRIMINALS--THAT'S ALL LANTERNS ARE!
BRR BRATTA BRATTA RATTATT T BRATTAT
I'M NO TRAITOR!
YOU ARE BETRAYING YOUR OWN PEOPLE!
WHOOOOOOM
HOLD IT RIGHT THERE, POOZERS.

TWENTY OF YOUSE AGAINST ONE LITTLE LADY LANTERN AIN'T FAIR.
WE'RE HER BUDDIES.
SO BACK OFF!
NO!
DON'T YOU SEE?
THIS WILL MAKE EVERYTHING WORSE!

YOU NEED A BIG LESSON ABOUT ATTACKIN' LANTERNS, POOZER.
MAYBE I'LL USE YOU AS A WARNIN' TO YOUR BUDDIES.

NO!
WE HAVE TO SHOW THAT WE PROTECT LIFE, NOT THREATEN IT.
YOU GIVIN' ME ORDERS NOW, NATU?

INSTRUCTOR KILOWOG--SIR--
IF WE WISH INNOCENT LIVES TO BE SPARED, I SUGGEST WE LEAVE THIS SITUATION TO COOL DOWN. ALL OF US.
HMMPH. YOU'RE RIGHT, PRINCESS. C'MON, NATU. OUT OF HERE.
NOW.

CLUSTRAL.

QUOND--GET THOSE STRANDS LINED UP. I'M BRINGING IN A BIG ONE.

WE'RE **BUSY** HERE. TELL HIM TO DO IT **HIMSELF.**

I--

GO ON, **TELL** HIM.

OR **ARE** YOU SCARED AFTER ALL?

I AIN'T SCARED. I--OKAY, YOU'RE **RIGHT**, I GUESS.

DO--DO IT YOURSELF, GARDNER. ME AND TANAK ARE BUSY.
WHAAAT?

BUSY? I'LL SHOW YOU BUSY!

C'MON, CAN'T YOU TAKE A JOKE? LEMME GO.
MAKE ME, FUNNY MAN.
ARE YOU CRAZY, GARDNER?
MAYBE YOU NEED SOME MORE SHORE LEAVE. LIKE FOR THE REST OF YOUR LIFE.
YOU TWO ARE THE ONES GONNA NEED TIME OFF--
--TO HEAL.

I OUGHTTA KNOCK THOSE STUPID GRINS OFF BOTH YOUR FACES.
NICE SHOW FOR THE LOCALS, GARDNER. REALLY GONNA MAKE 'EM RESPECT THE LANTERN CORPS.

BOOOM
THAT AND LETTING THEIR HOME GET MESSED UP SOME MORE.

I'LL DEAL WITH YOU CLOWNS LATER.
GARDNER'S SO DAMN CLEVER, LET HIM FINISH UP HERE HIMSELF.
BUT--

US TWO DID MOSTA THE WORK ANYWAY.
WE'RE GONNA GET INTO WORSE TROUBLE IF WE LEAVE, TANAK.
IF SALAAK--

NOW YOU'RE SCARED OF SALAAK?
LISTEN, GARDNER WOULD NEVER TAKE ANYTHIN' TO SALAAK--AND EVEN IF HE DID, SALAAK WOULD MORE'N LIKELY PUT HIM IN THE BRIG TOO.

C'MON, WE GOT BETTER THINGS TA DO THAN BE PUNCHING BAGS FOR THAT LOUD-MOUTH.
O-OKAY, TANAK...

SECTOR HOUSE 141.
SEEMS LIKE YOU GOT A PROBLEM DOWN THERE, NATU.
I PRESUME THAT IT'S THE KORUGARANS' INNATE DISTRUST OF THE LANTERN CORPS, INSTRUCTOR KILOWOG.
AND WHAT DO YOU KNOW ABOUT THAT, LANTERN IOLANDE?
AS A ROYAL PRINCESS, I TAKE A PARTICULAR INTEREST IN THE SOCIO-POLITICAL DIMENSION OF OUR ROLE. I HAVE READ EVERYTHING THAT IS AVAILABLE IN THE DATA BANKS.
GIVEN THE BEHAVIOR OF THE ROGUE KORUGARAN LANTERN, SINESTRO, THE SUSPICION WITH WHICH THE KORUGARANS VIEW OUR ACTIVITIES IS HARDLY SURPRISING. FURTHERMORE--
THERE'S NOTHING YOU CAN TEACH ME ABOUT KORUGARANS, THANKS.
ON THE CONTRARY, I FEEL THAT I MIGHT OFFER SOME USEFUL SUGGESTIONS, BASED ON MY RESEARCH, AS TO HOW YOU MIGHT BETTER INTEGRATE YOUR ROLE. FIRSTLY--
DIDN'T YOU HEAR ME, ROOKIE? I DON'T NEED YOUR INPUT!
REALLY.
THEN I SUPPOSE YOU KNOW EVERYTHING.
I KNOW MORE THAN YOU, SISTER.
AS A FELLOW LANTERN AND A ROYAL PRINCESS, I DEMAND THAT YOU TREAT ME WITH MORE RESPECT, LANTERN NATU.
YOU REALLY EXPECT ME TO PARTNER WITH THIS THIS BLUEBLOOD KNOW-IT-ALL, KILOWOG?

ENOUGH!

FROM *BOTH* OF YA.

I DON'T *CARE* WHO'S THE *BRAINIEST*.

I JUST CAME HERE TA *DELIVER* YA *NEW PARTNER*, NATU.

ALL *I* CARE ABOUT IS THAT YOU DO YOUR *DUTY*. IF YOUR *ARGUIN'* STOPS YOU DOIN' *THAT*, YOU'LL SEE JUST HOW *MUCH* I CARE.

AND *BELIEVE* ME, LADIES, THE WAY I BEEN *FEELIN'* LATELY, THAT'S SOMETHIN' YOU DON'T *WANNA* SEE.

NOW I'M GOIN' TO *MOGO*.

I'M *DUE* SOME R'N'R.

LANTERN NATU? I--
WELL, WHAT *IS* IT?

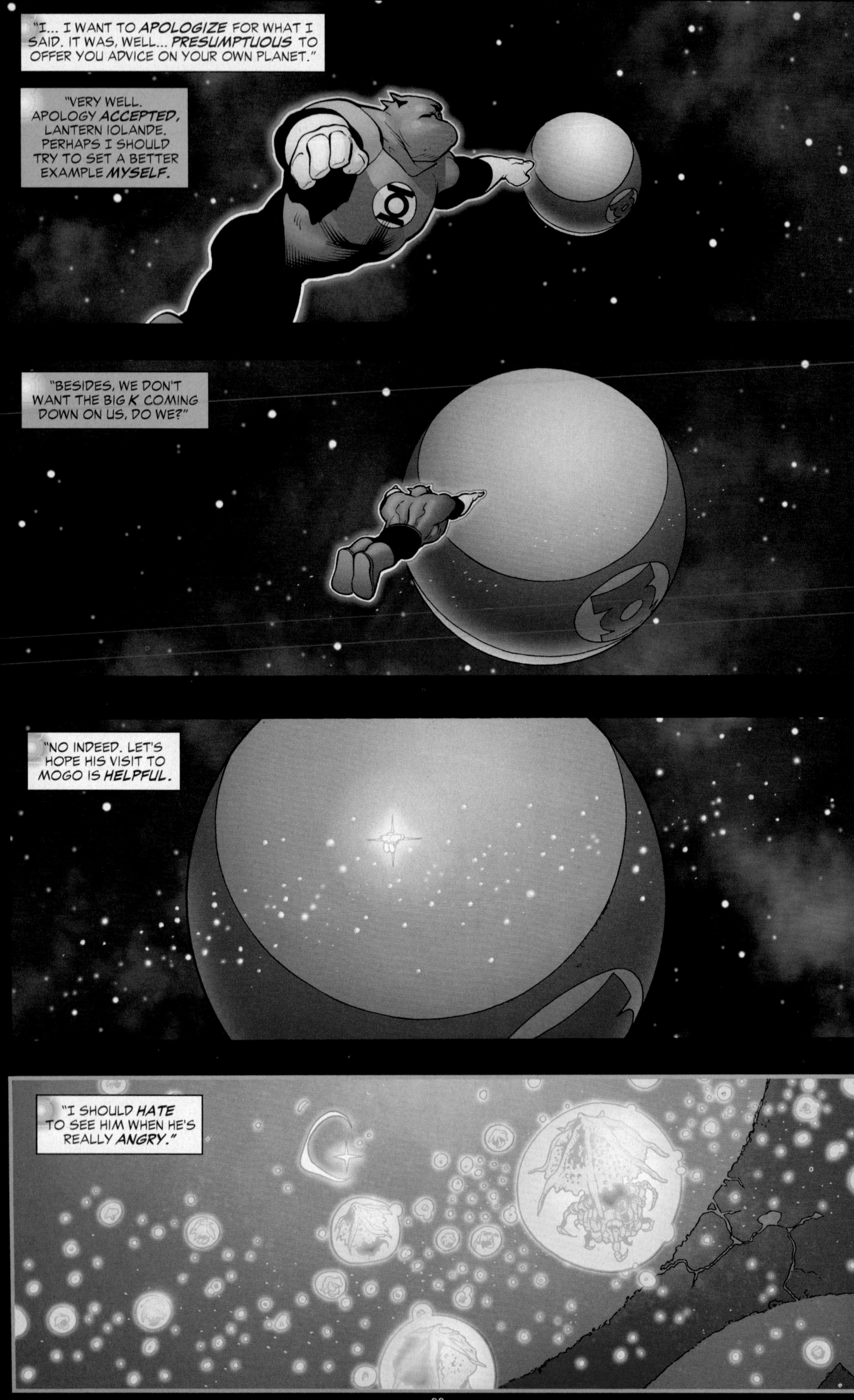
"I... I WANT TO APOLOGIZE FOR WHAT I SAID. IT WAS, WELL... PRESUMPTUOUS TO OFFER YOU ADVICE ON YOUR OWN PLANET."
"VERY WELL. APOLOGY ACCEPTED, LANTERN IOLANDE. PERHAPS I SHOULD TRY TO SET A BETTER EXAMPLE MYSELF.
"BESIDES, WE DON'T WANT THE BIG K COMING DOWN ON US, DO WE?"
"NO INDEED. LET'S HOPE HIS VISIT TO MOGO IS HELPFUL.
"I SHOULD HATE TO SEE HIM WHEN HE'S REALLY ANGRY."

GREEN LANTERN CORPS #11
Cover by Patrick Gleason, Christian Alamy and Moose Baumann

SECTOR 2684.
CLUSTRAL.
WHERE THE HELL IS EVERYONE?!
QUOND? TANAKATA Z? WHAT'S YOUR LOCATION? I NEED HELP HERE!
THE SECONDARY TREMORS ARE STARTIN' TO PULL SOME O' THESE MUDBALLS APART AGAIN.
THE PROPHECY
DAVE GIBBONS WRITER PATRICK GLEASON PENCILLER
PRENTIS ROLLINS INKER MOOSE BAUMANN COLORIST PHIL BALSMAN LETTERER

COME IN, YOU GOLDBRICKS!
WHERE IN SPACE ARE--
RELAX, GARDNER. WE'RE OKAY.
BETTER THAN OKAY.
WE'RE BACK AT OUR SECTOR HOUSE. FIGURED A BIG SHOT LIKE YOU COULD DEAL WITHOUT US. TELL 'EM, Q.
D-DIDN'T WANNA UPSET YOU AGAIN, LANTERN GARDNER.
YEAH, NO TELLING WHAT YOU MIGHT DO NEXT TIME YOU LOST IT.
WELL, YOU'RE BOTH GONNA FIND OUT.
ONCE I GET THIS SITUATION SQUARED AWAY, I'M COMIN' STRAIGHT TO YOUR SECTOR HOUSE--
AND KICKIN' YOUR SORRY BUTTS ALL THE WAY TO OA--AND A COURT-MARTIAL!

THERE IS NO NEED. I HAVE A NEAR-EIDETIC MEMORY, LANTERN NATU. NOT ONLY THAT, BUT--

I SAID RUN IT.

IN RESPECT OF YOUR RANK, THEN...

REPORTS FROM UNALIGNED MINING PLANET NIBELOS OF INCURSION BY THE CHILDREN OF THE WHITE LOBE, LAST KNOWN TO BE ACTIVE IN SECTOR 73. REPORT OF LANTERNS GARDNER AND CHTHO-CHTAS CHTHATIS STATES --

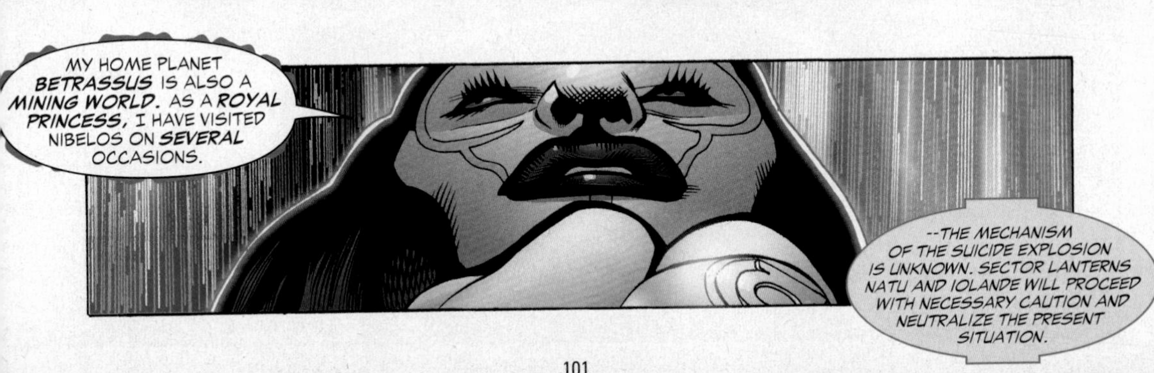

MY HOME PLANET BETRASSUS IS ALSO A MINING WORLD. AS A ROYAL PRINCESS, I HAVE VISITED NIBELOS ON SEVERAL OCCASIONS.
--THE MECHANISM OF THE SUICIDE EXPLOSION IS UNKNOWN. SECTOR LANTERNS NATU AND IOLANDE WILL PROCEED WITH NECESSARY CAUTION AND NEUTRALIZE THE PRESENT SITUATION.

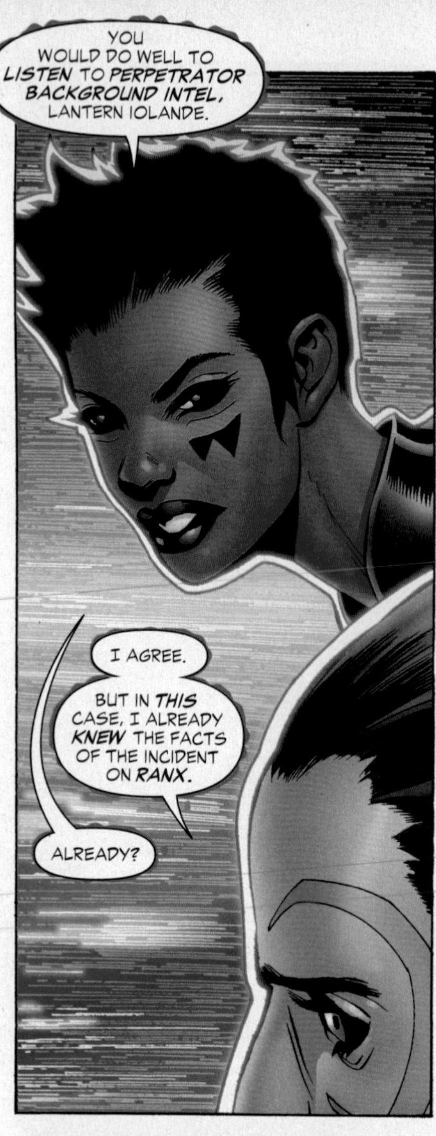

YOU WOULD DO WELL TO **LISTEN** TO **PERPETRATOR BACKGROUND INTEL,** LANTERN IOLANDE.
I AGREE.
BUT IN **THIS** CASE, I ALREADY **KNEW** THE FACTS OF THE INCIDENT ON **RANX.**
ALREADY?

IT WAS I WHO **ENTERED** THE DATA REGARDING THE **SUICIDE** OF THE KIDNAPPER ON RANX INTO THE SYSTEM, ON MY LAST **DUTY TURN.**
LEAVING TRANSLUMINAL. SHIELDS TO FORWARD.

AREN'T **YOU** A CLEVER GIRL?

THE **LOBE SPAWN** ARE NOT AFRAID TO **DIE,** ESPECIALLY IF THEY CAN TAKE A VICTIM **WITH** THEM.

YES, I **KNOW.** JUST MAKE SURE IT'S NOT **YOU,** IOLANDE.

SECTOR 3009.
LANTERN 2828? GREEN MAN?
GRATITUDE EXPRESSED FOR YOUR ATTENDANCE HERE ON INFORMAL ASSIGNMENT FROM YOUR HOME SECTOR.
ANOMALIES IN DATA FROM SUBJECT OF INVESTIGATION SEEMINGLY ILLOGICAL TO MY PROCESSORS. NON-LINEAR INPUT FROM YOUR ORGANIC INTUITION DEEMED ADVISABLE.
VESSEL IS OF UNKNOWN ORIGIN. NO SUCH DESIGN APPEARS ON UNIVERSAL IDENTIFICATION DATABASE.
DAMAGE APPEARS TO BE DELIBERATE. CAUSED BY FOCUSED YELLOW ENERGY.
MY MEMORY BANKS RECALL SIMILAR ACTIVITY BY THE ROGUE LANTERN SINESTRO. BUT...

CAUTION, 2828.
RING REPORTS INVERSE RADIATION READINGS, EXPLICABLE ONLY IF WRECK IS COMPOSED OF ANTI-MATTER.
CLOSE PROXIMITY TO NORMAL MATTER WILL PRECIPITATE MUTUALLY DESTRUCTIVE SUBATOMIC ANNULMENT.
2828? WHAT ARE YOU DOING?
ACTION ILLOGICAL. EXPLICABLE ONLY BY--
INSANITY.

MUTUALLY DESTRUCTIVE SUBATOMIC ANNULMENT.
BANG.

SECTOR 1417.
NIBELOS.
TZZAK TZZAK
TZZAK TZZAK
CHILDREN OF THE WHITE LOBE: PUT DOWN YOUR GUNS, I COMMAND YOU.
OUR WEAPONS ARE USELESS AGAINST THE LANTERN ENERGY.
TZZAK TZZAK
TZZAK TZZAK
BUT NOT AGAINST THESE ANIMALS!
COME ANY CLOSER, LANTERN--AND WE START KILLING THEM!
THOOOM
KILL THEM ALL!
NO.
NOT HERE.
NOT TODAY.
TZZAK
TZZAK

NOW PUT THOSE GUNS DOWN BEFORE SOMEONE LOSES AN EYE.
WE DO NOT FEAR DEATH FOR THE GLORY OF OUR CAUSE, LANTERN!
FINE BY ME.
BUT FIRST YOU'VE GOT QUESTIONS TO ANSWER.
HOLD STILL AND I'LL CUT THOSE CHAINS.
WHAT'S IN HERE THAT'S SO PRECIOUS TO THESE MANIACS?
IT'S TELLURIUM, FOUND ONLY ON NIBELOS.
IT HAS THE UNIQUE PROPERTY OF BEING ABLE TO TRANSMUTE MENTAL ENERGY INTO HEAT.
THE BOX IS SOLID ANGRATITE, A DENSE INSULATOR USED TO PROTECT THE TELLURIUM FROM STRAY MENTAL ENERGIES.
SUFFICIENT CONCENTRATION OF PSYCHIC ENERGY COULD--
SORANIK! GET RID OF THE NUGGET! IT--

DOWN!

BOOOM

IT'S CLEAR NOW. THESE MUTANTS DISPLAY HYPERDEVELOPMENT OF THE FRONTAL LOBE.
THE INCREASED MENTAL ENERGY ENABLES EXPLOSIVE SUPER-HEATING OF THE TELLURIUM.
WHICH EXPLAINS THE REPORT FROM RANX.
IF THEY IMPLANT TELLURIUM INSIDE THEMSELVES, THEY BECOME LIVING BOMBS.

IS THIS ALL THE TELLURIUM THE MINERS HAVE EXTRACTED?
OH NO. THESE ARE BUT TRADE SAMPLES.
THE MAIN TELLURIUM MINE IS ON THE OTHER SIDE OF NIBELOS.

THEN WE HAVE TO GO MINING--
YES. OF COURSE.

SECTOR 2261.

MOGO.

I'M TIRED, SO TIRED.
THE CORPS. THE CORPS HAS DONE THIS TO YOU, KILOWOG.

NO.
YOU GAVE THEM EVERYTHING YOU HAD. YOUR STRENGTH, YOUR WILL.
THE CORPS IS MY FAMILY.

YOU LEFT THE MASS-MIND OF BOLOVAX FOR THE CORPS. YOU LEFT YOUR SOUL MATE. EVERYONE YOU REALLY LOVED. EVERYONE WHO REALLY LOVED YOU.
THE GUARDIANS DON'T LOVE YOU. THEY USE YOU. USE YOUR GREAT POWERS TO TRAIN THEIR PUPPETS.

NO. THE CORPS. THEY'RE MY BROTHERS.
NO. THEY FEAR YOU. THEY OBEY YOU. THEY DON'T LOVE YOU. NOT LIKE US.

YOU? BUT YOU'RE DEAD. ALL DEAD.
NO. WE LIVE. AS LONG AS YOU LIVE, SO DO WE.
LOOK CLOSER, KILOWOG.

WE ARE BOLOVAX. WE ARE YOUR BLOOD, YOUR MIND, YOUR SPIRIT. YOU ARE ONE WITH US.
WE LOVE YOU, KILOWOG.

BUT WE HATE THE GUARDIANS. WE HATE THEM FOR WHAT THEY HAVE DONE TO YOU. WHAT THEY HAVE TAKEN FROM YOU.
AND WE HATE THEM FOR TAKING YOU FROM US.
YES. TAKEN.
YOU ARE TIRED, WE KNOW. BUT WE CAN GIVE YOU NEW STRENGTH. THE STRENGTH OF OUR COMMON WILL. USE IT.

USE IT TO DESTROY THE GUARDIANS. AND THEIR HATEFUL PUPPETS.
YES.
THEN COME BACK TO US, BACK TO BOLOVAX, WHERE YOU CAN REST IN OUR LOVE. FOREVER.

YES.
FOREVER.

SECTOR 2682
RANAGAR CITY, RANN.

SO, YOU'RE A SOLDIER?
WAS.
BEEN OFF-WORLD A WHILE.
THE RANN/THAN WAR.

THAT WHERE YOU GOT THE SCAR?
NAH.
GOT THAT BEFORE I JOINED.

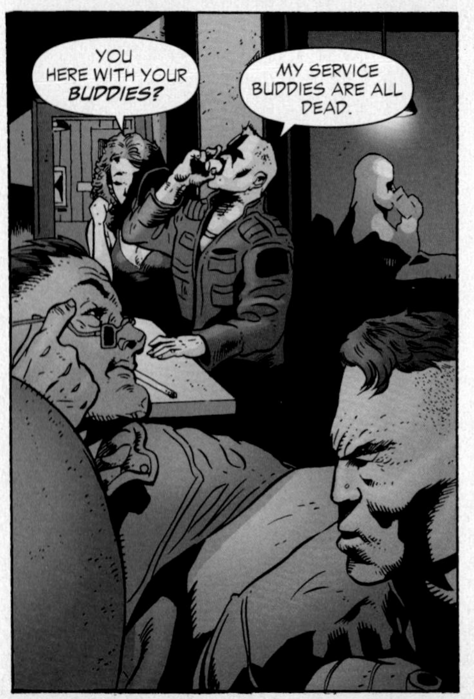
YOU HERE WITH YOUR BUDDIES?
MY SERVICE BUDDIES ARE ALL DEAD.

ENOUGH QUESTIONS.
WHAT SAY WE TAKE A WALK? SOMEWHERE MORE--
PLACE NOT GOOD ENOUGH FOR YOU, PAL?

YOU ARMY GUYS THINK YOU CAN JUST COME IN HERE AND HELP YOURSELVES TO OUR WOMEN?
I'M NOT IN THE ARMY.
THEN WHAT? SPACE NAVY?
PLANETARY MARINES?
I'M IN THE CORPS--
YOU REALLY WANNA KNOW?
WHAMM
THE GREEN LANTERN CORPS!

HATE TO BREAK UP THE LOVE FEST.
C'MON, BUDDY. **HOME TIME.**

YOU GOT A **THANAGARIAN** FOR A BUDDY?
THEY **WIPED OUT** HALF MY **FAMILY!**
I GET MY HANDS ON **YOU**, I'LL GIVE YOU **ANOTHER** SCAR!

LIZARD LOVER!

WOMEN, EH?
HMMPH.
MAYBE I NEED ANOTHER TRIP TO **MOGO.**

OA
PLANETARY CITADEL OF THE GUARDIANS OF THE UNIVERSE.
COUNTLESS EONS AGO, WE PURGED THEM FROM THE STARWAYS.
ENTOMBED THEM ON YSMAULT. CHAINED THE REGENTS OF THE EMPIRE OF TEARS TO THE CORPSE-WORLD WHICH SPAWNED THEM.
FORBADE ALL CONTACT WITH THEM.

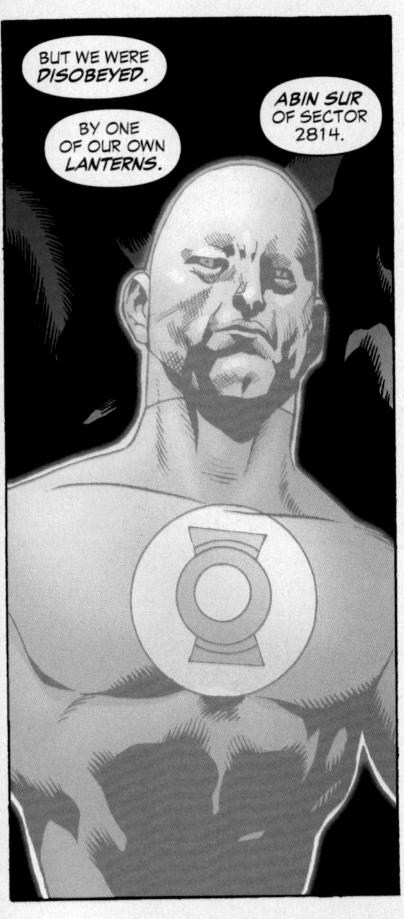
BUT WE WERE DISOBEYED.
BY ONE OF OUR OWN LANTERNS.
ABIN SUR OF SECTOR 2814.

ABIN SUR? BUT HE WAS ONE OF THE MOST TRUSTWORTHY AND VENERATED LANTERNS OF ALL.
HE ACTED IN GOOD FAITH, TO SAVE A LIFE...
BUT IN SO DOING, HE WAS LED TOWARDS HIS OWN DEMISE.

THE REGENT QULL OF THE FIVE INVERSIONS WHISPERED MALIGN PROPHECIES TO HIM.
PLANTED IN HIM AN INSIDIOUS FEAR OF THE FUTURE. CAUSED HIM TO DIE, YEARS LATER, BECAUSE HE DOUBTED THE POWER OF HIS RING.
HMM. SUCH ARE THE PERILS OF BEING A LANTERN.

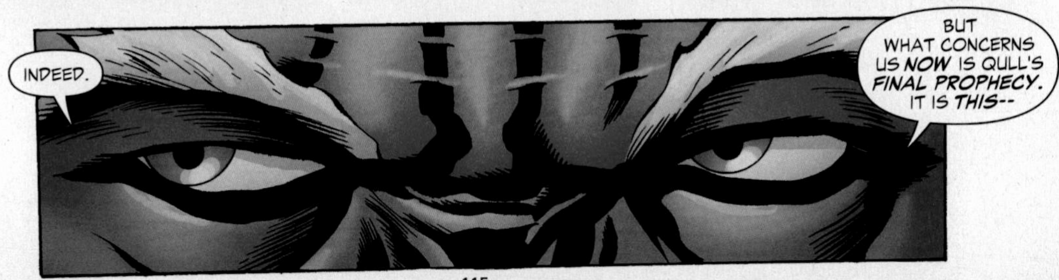
INDEED.
BUT WHAT CONCERNS US NOW IS QULL'S FINAL PROPHECY. IT IS THIS--

"AFTER UNTOLD MILLENNIA, THE ENEMIES OF THE GREEN LANTERN CORPS WILL RISE UNITED AGAINST THEM.
"THE CORPS SHALL BE DESTROYED TO THE LAST LIFE FORM. THE PLANET OA SHALL BE AS DUST.
"AMONG THE GATHERED FOEMEN SHALL BE NUMBERED THE WEAPONERS OF QWARD, RANX THE SENTIENT CITY, AND THE UNSPEAKABLE CHILDREN OF THE WHITE LOBE.
"THE EMPIRE OF TEARS, FINALLY RELEASED FROM ENTOMBMENT, SHALL JOIN THE ASSAULT.
"SODAM YAT, A DAXAMITE HAILED AS THE ULTIMATE GREEN LANTERN, WILL PERISH BATTLING THE LOBE-SPAWN.
"THE PLANET-FORM MOGO WILL BE THE LAST TO FALL, AS RANX EXPLODES A BLINK BOMB WITHIN HIS CORE.
"AND AFTER THAT..."

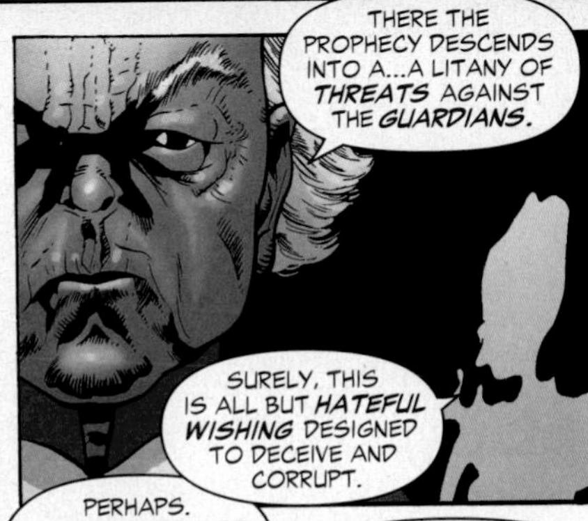
THERE THE PROPHECY DESCENDS INTO A...A LITANY OF THREATS AGAINST THE GUARDIANS.
SURELY, THIS IS ALL BUT HATEFUL WISHING DESIGNED TO DECEIVE AND CORRUPT.

PERHAPS. BUT THAT ABIN SUR WAS DRIVEN TO HIS DEATH PROVES HOW POISONOUS SUCH WORDS ARE, REAL OR NOT.
AND MANY RACES POSSESS PRECOGNITIVE ABILITIES TO VARYING DEGREES. WE CANNOT DISMISS THESE PREDICTIONS.

ALREADY WE HAVE NOTED A RESURGENCE OF ACTIVITY BY THE CHILDREN OF THE WHITE LOBE.
AND RANX HAS ONCE AGAIN OPPOSED OUR LANTERNS.
THESE ACTIVITIES MAY BE COINCIDENTAL, BUT THEY MAY NOT.
YOU WILL WATCH AND REPORT TO US ANY ACTIVITY THAT LENDS CREDENCE TO THIS PROPHECY.

BUT LISTEN WELL, SALAAK. YOU WILL TELL NO OTHER BEING OF THIS.
REMEMBER ABIN SUR.
NOW, LEAVE US.

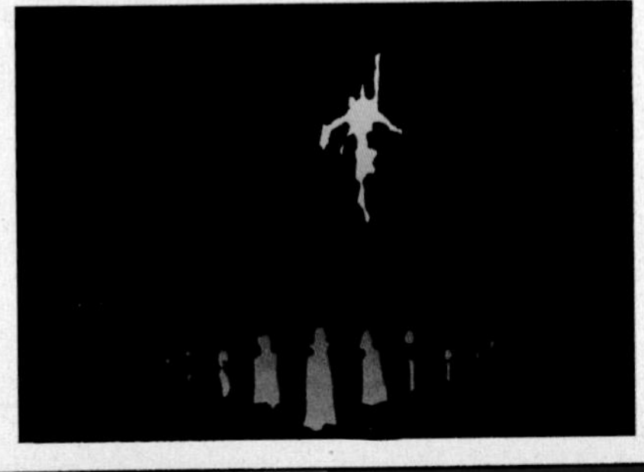

HEY, BIG GUY!
COME AND JOIN US!

KILOWOG! OVER HERE...
DOESN'T SEEM HIS NORMAL HAPPY SELF.
WE'VE ALL BEEN UNDER A LOT O' PRESSURE TRAINING THE NEW RECRUITS. BUT NONE AS MUCH AS HIM...

AH, LET THE POOZER EAT IN PEACE.
SO, BRIK, WHAT'S THAT RUMOR ABOUT SALAAK'S SHORE LEAVE?

SEEMS HE BAILED GARDNER OUT ON SOME PLEASURE PLANET AND THEN HE AND THESE TWO--
SSSHT.

MAYBE HIS HIGHNESS WOULD LIKE TO TELL US HIMSELF.
HIM? NAH, HE'S ZIPPED TIGHT AS A BANANA.
BESIDES, WE'D ALL HAVE WOUND UP WITH INDIGESTION TRYIN' NOT TO LAUGH.

GOT TO THINKIN' HOW DEEP *IN* YOU ARE, EH?

SECTOR HOUSE 268 PROXIMAL.
SECURITY SCAN DETECTED. RESPONDING.
WELL, ***DADDY'S*** HOME, BOYS--

--AND HE'S GONNA GIVE YOU THE ***WHUPPIN'*** O' YOUR ***LIVES!***
HONOR LANTERN GUY GARDNER. AUTHENTICATED. ENTRY AUTHORIZED.

OKAY, SHOW YOURSELVES. I KNOW YOU'RE *IN* HERE.

--ME.

Cover by Patrick Gleason, Wayne Faucher and Moose Baumann

GUESS MOGO'S ANGER MANAGEMENT MUSTA DONE YOU SOME GOOD.
YOU ONLY BARELY LOST IT BACK THERE ON RANN.

LEAVING TRANSLUMINAL. SECTOR HOUSE 268 PROXIMAL.
AND YOU DIDN'T EVEN SPEAK TO MOGO?
I TOLD YOU, ONCE THE HORMONE SURGE HAD PASSED, QALYRA MEANT LESS TO ME THAN A...A COLD BREW.

BUT NEXT CYCLE, I'M MAKIN' SURE I'M NEAR SOME LIZARKON HONEY WITH NO DISTRACTIONS, YOU BET.

SECURITY SCAN DETECTED. RESPONDING.

LANTERNS VATH SARN AND ISAMOT KOL. AUTHENTICATED. ENTRY AUTHORIZED.

ANYBODY HOME?
LOOKS LIKE SOMEONE'S IN THE REC ROOM.
PROBABLY THAT LAZY WISE ASS QUOND. GONNA BE AN AGE BEFORE HIS RING

--CHARGE.
HONOR LANTERN GARDNER?
FUGITIVE
AVE GIBBONS writer PATRICK GLEASON & TOM NGUYEN pencillers PRENTISS ROLLINS & TOM NGUYEN inkers
MOOSE BAUMANN colorist PHIL BALSMAN letterer

HELP ME HERE.
THIS ONE'S STILL ALIVE.
VITAL SIGNS SLOWING. BRAIN ACTIVITY ERRATIC.
TANAK? WHO DID THIS?

HE DID.
HE KILLED US.
HE? WHO ARE YOU TALKING ABOUT, BUDDY?
HIM. G--

G-GUY GARDNER. HE D-DID IT.
HE...HE K-KILLED US...

VITAL SIGNS ABSENT.
SUBJECT DECEASED.

A PRISON OF *ANGRATITE* FOR YOU--

AND A SHIELD OF LANTERN ENERGY FOR *YOU!*

WH-WHERE DID YOU GET SO MUCH ANGRATITE?
WE LOCATED AND EXCAVATED IT WITH OUR POWER RINGS. LANTERN NATU HAD THE IDEA OF CONSTRUCTING A CONTAINER OF ANGRATITE TO INSULATE THE PSYCHOACTIVE TELLURIUM...
...BUT, SINCE WE COULD NOT INSULATE EVERY PIECE OF TELLURIUM IN THE MINE, WE INSULATED THE SOURCE OF THE BRAINWAVES INSTEAD.
THAT WAS MY IDEA.
I DON'T THINK THEY'RE INTERESTED IN WHOSE IDEA THIS WAS, LANTERN IOLANDE.
WHOOOM
WHA--?
THEY'RE ALL DEAD.
YOU HARDLY NEED BE A DOCTOR TO KNOW THAT. AND WE SPOKE OF THE POSSIBILITY THAT THE CHILDREN OF THE WHITE LOBE MIGHT ALREADY BE CARRYING TELLURIUM.
LIKE THEIR KINSWOMAN ON RANX, THEY CHOOSE DEATH BEFORE CAPTURE.
AT LEAST WE HAVE THE CHILDREN WE CAPTURED EARLIER TO TAKE BACK TO OA FOR INTERR--
URGENT PERSONAL MESSAGE RECEIVED.

URGENT PERSONAL MESSAGE RECEIVED.
TAKE IT.
IT'S JUST A DISTRACTION IF YOU DON'T.
I'M GOING TO SEAL THIS MINE ON BEHALF OF THE GUARDIANS AND RE-BURY ANY TELLURIUM ORE YOU'VE ALREADY EXTRACTED.
NOTHING MOVES ON OR OFF THIS WORLD WITHOUT EXPRESS PERMISSION FROM OA.
BUT, OUR TRADE--
THERE ARE NO BUTS. UNTIL THE THREAT FROM THE WHITE LOBE IS NEUTRALIZED, YOU'RE UNDER OUR--
LANTERN NATU.
I HAVE TO GO. RETURN HOME TO BETRASSUS.
O HOME? WE AVE A MISSION COMPLETE. YOU N'T JUST LEAVE WHENEV--
MY FATHER. THE KING. THEY SAY HE--HE'S DYING...
I SEE. GO THEN, WITH MY PERMISSION.
ALTHOUGH I SUSPECT

SECTOR HOUSE 268.
YOU DON'T BELIEVE I KILLED THEM, DO YA? HE WAS DELIRIOUS, BRAIN-DAMAGED.
I BEEN IN THIS CORPS SINCE YOU GRUNTS WERE STILL IN DIAPERS. I'M NO LANTERN-KILLER.
THEY WERE ALREADY LAYIN' THERE WHEN I ARRIVED.
WHAT DO THEIR RING LOGS SAY?
RECENTLY? TANAKATA Z VISITS MOGO, WHILE QUOND'S HANGIN' OUT HERE, THEN THEY'RE IN THE LUSTRAL SYSTEM--WITH HONOR LANTERN GARDNER--THEN THEY COME BACK HERE...
AND THEN THE RING LOGS BOTH GO BLANK. THEY BEEN WIPED.
YOU, UH, GET ON ALL RIGHT WITH THEM OUT IN LUSTRAL?
DON'T LIKE YOUR TONE, SON.
YOU LIKE ANOTHER SCAR?
LOOK, THESE QUESTIONS ARE GONNA BE ASKED, EVEN IF NOT BY US, HONOR LANTERN.
CHECK OUT THE SECTOR HOUSE ENTRY AND EXIT LOG. THE PERP WILL BE IN THERE.
THAT WAS NEXT.
VATH.
GET THE MOST RECENT INS AND OUTS.

WAS EMPTY WHEN TANAKATA Z AND QUOND ARRIVED.
PRIOR EMERGENCY IN 2681 SUMMONED ALL AVAILABLE LANTERNS.
GARDNER ARRIVED.
YOU AND ME, ISAMOT.

LOOKS LIKE YOU WERE HERE ALONE WITH THEM WHEN THEY WERE ATTACKED, GARDNER.
I'M SORRY, HONOR LANTERN. WE NEED TO ESCORT YOU BACK TO OA SO YOU CAN TALK THIS OUT.
AND... WE'LL NEED YOUR RING.

OKAY, BUT--

--YOU'LL HAVE TO TAKE IT FROM ME!

AFTER HIM, DAMMIT!

THIS IS HONOR LANTERN GARDNER OVERRIDING SECTOR HOUSE CENTRAL COMPUTER.
EMERGENCY SITUATION. LOCK DOWN THE FACILITY.

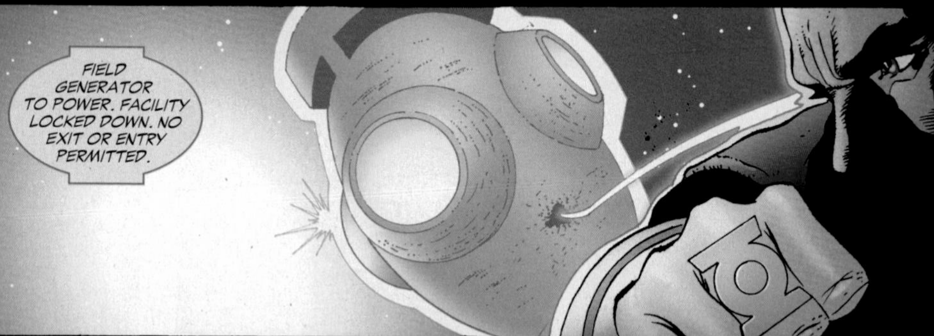
FIELD GENERATOR TO POWER. FACILITY LOCKED DOWN. NO EXIT OR ENTRY PERMITTED.

DAMMIT. HE'S GETTIN' AWAY!
GUESS HE'S NOT AN HONOR LANTERN FOR NOTHIN'.
NO ENTRY OR EXIT PERMITTED. AUTHORIZATION FROM OA REQUIRED TO UNLOCK FACILITY.

NOW WHAT?
WE CONTACT OA. THEN WE GET ON HIS TRAIL.
I MAY NOT BE AN HONOR LANTERN, BUT I GOT A GOOD IDEA WHERE HE'S HEADED.

OA.
LANTERN HAZARD SIMULATION FACILITY.
THE RECRUITS SEEM UP TO STANDARD, DON'T YOU THINK, KILOWOG?
NOT MY STANDARD. THEY'RE CLUMSY AND SLOPPY, SALAAK.
YOUR SOJOURN ON MOGO SEEMS TO HAVE DONE LITTLE TO IMPROVE YOUR MOOD, KILOWOG.

PROTOCOL OFFICER SALAAK. 3009 DEBRIEFING COMMENCING IN FIVE.
ON MY WAY.
I'LL LEAVE YOU TO CONDUCT THE REMAINDER OF THE TRAINING REVIEW YOURSELF, KILOWOG.
WATCH WHERE YOU'RE GOIN', YAT!
S-SORRY...
YOU WILL BE, YA RETTIN' POOZER! DOUBLE FATIGUE DUTY FOR YOU AND A WASHOUT IF IT HAPPENS AGAIN!
LANTERN DEBRIEFING FACILITY.
...ANTIMATTER DEBRIS.
A SHIP OR SOME OTHER KIND OF ARTIFACT?
NO.
JUST DEBRIS.
LANTERN STEL GOT TOO CLOSE. I WARNED HIM, BUT...

WHAT DOES HIS RING SAY?
NOTHIN' MUCH. MAINLY STATIC. ANTIMATTER RADIATION MUSTA SCRAMBLED IT.
ACCIDENT? IT HAPPENS. PLENTY OF WANDERING JUNK OUT THERE BETWEEN THE STARS.
AGREED?
AGREED. RETURN TO DUTY, LANTERN 2828.
SORRY ABOUT STEL, 2828. HE'LL BE MISSED.
YEAH. THE OL' TINCAN HAD A HEART O' GOL--
ALERT. ALERT.
LANTERNS DOWN.
LANTERNS DOWN.
LANTERN VATH SARN REPORTS TWO FATALITIES AT SECTOR HOUSE 268.
PATCH ME THROUGH TO THE SECTOR HOUSE.
AS IF WE HAVEN'T HAD ENOUGH DEATH FOR ONE DAY.

BETRASSUS.
MY LORD KING, I FEAR YOUR END IS NEAR.
I...KNOW.
IOLANDE... COME...COME CLOSER...
WITH YOUR...YOUR BROTHERS GONE, YOU ARE THE ONLY... HOPE OF THE LINE OF BETRA...
GIVE UP THE LANTERN CORPS...AND RULE HERE AS A QUEEN.
FATHER. I --I CANNOT... I HAVE MY DUTY TO THE CORPS--
DO... AS I SAY, GIRL ...*KOF*...RULE BETRASSUS... THAT IS YOUR DUTY...
CAN'T YOU HELP HIM, DOCTOR? GIVE ME TIME TO THINK?
MY LADY, I FEAR I CAN BUT EASE THE KING'S SUFFERING. I CAN BUY HIM NO MORE TIME.
PRINCESS--
LET ME TAKE A LOOK AT YOUR FATHER.

SECTOR 2261.
MOGO.
WHAT AILS YOU, BROTHER GARDNER?
I'M IN TROUBLE, MOGO.
AGAIN?

NO, REAL TROUBLE. I BEEN ACCUSED OF MURDER.
MURDER? OF WHOM?
A LANTERN.
QUOND OF SECTOR 2684.

AND WHO ACCUSES YOU?

HIS PARTNER. TANAKATA Z.
HE'S DEAD NOW TOO.
AND HOW CAN I HELP YOU, BROTHER GARDNER?

FIRST OFF, BY BELIEVIN' I DIDN'T DO IT. THEN BY GIVIN' ME SOME INFO.
TANAKATA Z VISITED YOU JUST BEFORE ALL THIS.
I WANNA KNOW IF HE WAS ACTING STRANGE. IF THERE WAS ANYTHIN' YOU KNEW THAT MIGHT ACCOUNT FOR HIM ACCUSIN' ME.
TRUTH IS, I DON'T HAVE ANY OTHER LEADS, AND PRETTY SOON THE WHOLE CORPS IS GONNA BE ON MY TAIL.

MANY VISIT MOGO.
COME, SHELTER IN MY FOREST. REST, WHILE I THINK.

TANAKATA Z... YES. HE HAD SEEN SOME HORRORS IN THE PROCYON SYSTEM AND NEEDED TO TALK. HE LEFT, AT PEACE ONCE MORE.
NO REASON WHY HE SHOULD FALSELY ACCUSE YOU OF MURDER.

SO MUCH FOR THAT LEAD.
I BETTER GO.
WAIT, BROTHER GARDNER. ARE YOU SURE YOU DO NOT NEED TO TALK MORE?

WHAT ARE YOU SAYING, MOGO? YOU THINK I REALLY DID KILL THEM?
JUST STOP AND TALK FOR A WHILE. TALK TO ONE WHO KNOWS YOU WELL.

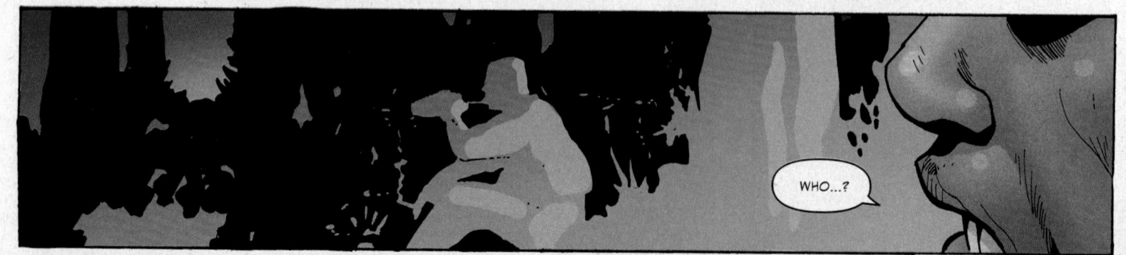
WHO...?

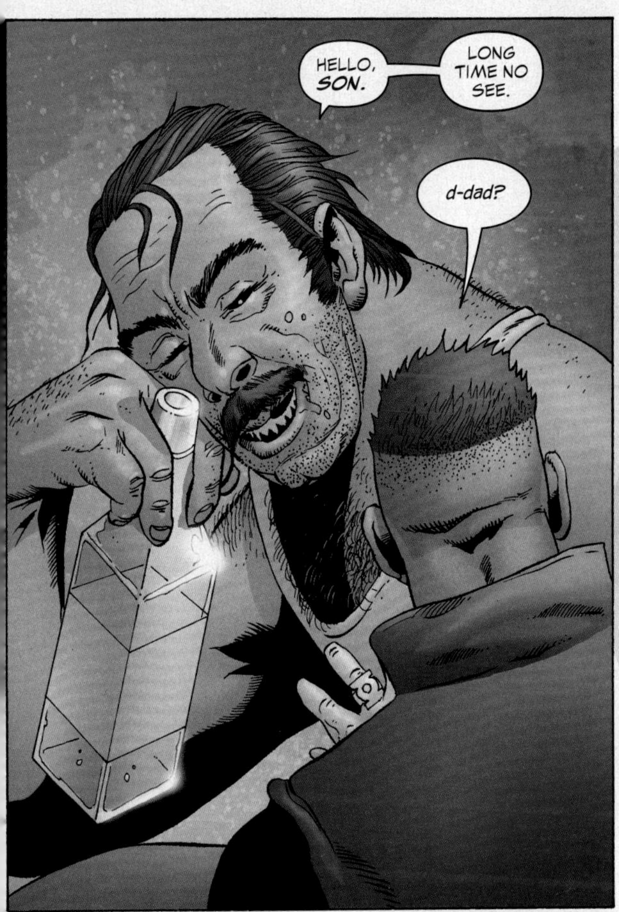
HELLO, SON.
LONG TIME NO SEE.
d-dad?

YOU'VE GONE AN' DONE IT THIS TIME, SON. THIS IS ONE FIX YOU AIN'T GETTIN' OUT OF.
STILL, YA NEVER WERE ANY GOOD. NO MATTER HOW HARD I TRIED TO BEAT THE BAD OUTTA YA.
MEBBE I SHOULD TRY AGAIN.

C'MERE, YA LITTLE RUNT!
DON'T KNOW WHY YOU'RE PLAYIN' THESE MIND GAMES, MOGO, BUT I AIN'T GOT TIME.
I'M LEAVIN'. RIGHT NOW.

THUMP
NNNNF

MOGO! STOP THIS...

BETRASSUS.
HOW MUCH LONGER MUST WE WAIT?
WE ARE ALL ANXIOUS, YOUR HIGHNESS...
BUT IT IS RIGHT THAT WE LEAVE THE DOCTORS TO THEIR WORK, AS THEY INSTRUCTED.
PERHAPS WE MIGHT JOIN TOGETHER IN PRAYER?
NO.
DOCTORS AND PRIESTS DO NOT GIVE ORDERS TO PRINCESSES.
I WILL SEE WHAT THEY ARE--
KLIK
FATHER?
I'M SORRY, IOLANDE.
THERE WAS NOTHING WE COULD DO.
WHAT?

CALL YOURSELF A DOCTOR?
PRINCESS... Y-YOUR HIGHNESS. DOCTOR NATU DID ALL THAT--
YOU LET MY FATHER DIE.
WITH HIM DEAD, THIS PLANET WILL DESCEND INTO CHAOS.
AND IT WILL ALL BE YOUR FAULT.
MY FAULT? LET ME TELL YOU SOMETHING--
I'M THE BEST DOCTOR IN THIS SECTOR, PERHAPS IN THE WHOLE GALAXY.
IF I COULDN'T SAVE HIM, HE COULDN'T BE SAVED.
I'VE TAKEN ENOUGH BLAME IN MY LIFE.
THIS IS YOUR PLANET. YOU DEAL WITH IT.
I HAVE WORK TO DO ON KORUGAR.

OA.
...LANTERN GARDNER THEN USED HIS SENIORITY TO LOCK DOWN SECTOR HOUSE 284 AND ESCAPE.

GARDNER IS A HOTHEAD, BUT HE WOULDN'T KILL ANOTHER LANTERN.
YOU SPEAK TRUE. HE WOULD NEVER ACT SO.

EVEN I, WHO NEEDS NO REMINDING OF HIS WAYS, CANNOT BELIEVE THAT HE WOULD DO THIS. HOWEVER...
THE EVIDENCE IS STRONG. THE DEATH STATEMENT OF LANTERN TANAKATA Z, WITNESSED BY TWO LANTERNS, IS POWERFUL.
WE MUST QUESTION LANTERN GARDNER IMMEDIATELY.

AGREED. WE SHOULD APPREHEND HIM, BRING HIM BACK TO OA, AND GIVE HIM THE CHANCE TO EXPLAIN.
EXPLAIN? EXPLAIN?

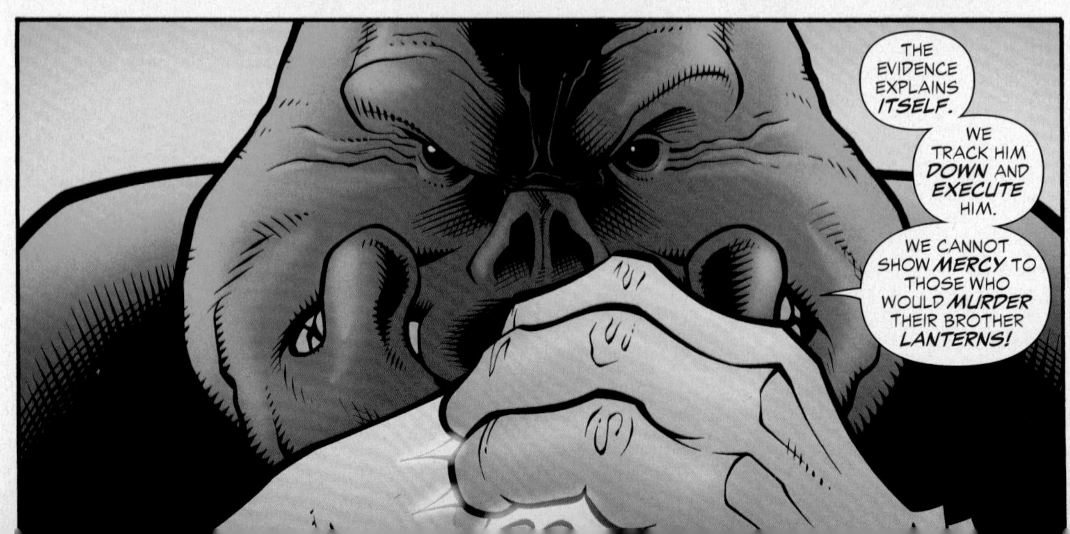
THE EVIDENCE EXPLAINS ITSELF.
WE TRACK HIM DOWN AND EXECUTE HIM.
WE CANNOT SHOW MERCY TO THOSE WHO WOULD MURDER THEIR BROTHER LANTERNS!

A MAD DOG SHOULD BE KILLED BEFORE IT CAN ATTACK AGAIN.
IF NO ONE ELSE HERE HAS THE GUTS FOR IT, SEND ME.
THERE WILL BE NO MORE TALK OF KILLING, KILOWOG. YOU KNOW WELL THAT THE GUARDIANS FORBID SUCH SUMMARY PUNISHMENT.
BEFORE WE CAN ARREST GARDNER, WE HAVE TO FIND HIM.

REPORTING LANTERNS VATH SARN AND ISAMOT KOL SUSPECT THAT GARDNER HAS GONE TO MOGO. DECEASED LANTERN TANAKATA Z HAD RECENTLY VISITED THERE FOR ROUTINE COUNSELING.
THEY BELIEVE GARDNER MIGHT SEEK TO PROVE HIMSELF INNOCENT WITH POSSIBLE PROOF OF TANAKATA Z'S MENTAL INSTABILITY PROVIDED BY MOGO.

WHAT ARE YOU SAYING?
THAT TANAK KILLED QUOND AND THEN HIMSELF TO FRAME GARDNER?
PAH! THIS IS MADNESS!

IT MAY BE BUT--
WAIT. I HAVE NEW INFORMATION.
MOGO HIMSELF IS ONLINE...HE REPORTS THE PRESENCE OF LANTERN GARDNER IN HIS FORESTS.
IN WHICH CASE, MOGO CAN DETAIN HIM UNTIL LANTERNS SARN AND KOL ARRIVE. IT IS THEIR CASE, BY RIGHT.

TWO ROOKIES TO TAKE AN HONOR LANTERN? THAT IS MADNESS TOO. I SHOULD GO, I TELL YOU.
THEY ARE NO LONGER ROOKIES.
AND I WILL ORDER MOGO'S SECTOR PARTNER LANTERN TO ASSIST THEM...

SO WHERE IS HE, DAMMIT?
MOGO?
GOT A FEELING HE'S RIGHT BEHIND US, BUDDY...
I MEAN HIS PARTNER. AND YOU KNOW IT.
RING? REPORT ON PROXIMITY OF LANTERN 2261-- NOT THE PLANET-SIZED ONE.
LANTERN APPROACHING, DISTANCE ONE HUNDRED KLICKS.
HUH? A HUNDRED KLICKS? WE SHOULD SEE HIM BY NOW, DAMMIT.
WE DO.
LOOK.

GREETINGS, LANTERNS VATH AND ISAMOT. I AM LANTERN BZZD OF APIATON.
MY APOLOGIES FOR THE DELAY. I WAS ACROSS THE SECTOR. SPACE PIRATES, YOU KNOW...
I AM SORRY TO WELCOME YOU TO SECTOR 2261 ON SUCH AN UNPLEASANT MISSION.
NOW, LET US WASTE NO MORE TIME.
WE'RE TRACKING ONE OF THE MOST POWERFUL, RESOURCEFUL LANTERNS THERE IS, ON THE RUN FOR MURDER, AND THEY SEND US A GNAT?
SCALE IS ONLY RELATIVE, LANTERN VATH.
AFTER ALL, YOU ARE SMALLER TO MOGO THAN I AM TO YOU.
AND BE ASSURED, MY WILL IS JUST AS STRONG AS YOURS.
AS IS MY RESOLVE TO BRING EVIL TO JUSTICE.

GREEN LANTERN CORPS #13
Cover by Patrick Gleason, Christian Alamy and Moose Baumann

SECTOR 2261.
MOGO.
MY PARTNER MOGO IS VERY LARGE. I SUGGEST WE START OUR SEARCH FOR THE FUGITIVE IN THE THERAPY AREA OF HIS FORESTS.
IT IS WHERE HONOR LANTERN GARDNER WAS LAST REPORTED BY MOGO.
WHAT'S TO SAY HE'LL STILL BE THERE?
MOGO CAN BE VERY HOSPITABLE AND PERSUASIVE.
SO, WE GONNA SPLIT UP? WE CAN SEARCH QUICKER THAT WAY.
NO OFFENSE, ISAMOT KOL, BUT THIS IS AN HONOR LANTERN WE SEEK. HE HAS ALREADY ESCAPED FROM YOU TWO.
WITH MY ASSISTANCE, IF WE STICK TOGETHER, WE MAY BE ABLE TO TAKE HIM THIS TIME.
I GUESS EVERY LITTLE BIT HELPS.
ER, NO OFFENSE, LANTERN BZZD.

NONE TAKEN, VATH SARN. NONE TAKEN.
OKAY. NOW THAT WE'RE ALL BUDDIES, LET'S GET STARTED.
WAIT!
IT SEEMS WE DO NOT NEED TO PURSUE LANTERN GARDNER--
--HE'S HEADING STRAIGHT FOR US.
HOLD IT RIGHT THERE, GARDNER. WE'RE TAKING YOU IN.
FOR THE MURDER OF LANTERNS TANAKATA Z AND QUOND.
HAND OVER YOUR RING.
NEVER.
I DONE SOME EDGY THINGS IN MY TIME--
THOOM
--BUT MURDER ISN'T ONE OF 'EM!

LISTEN, THERE'S SOMETHING SCREWY GOIN' ON WITH MOGO!
INSTEAD OF FIXIN' LANTERNS, HE'S BRAINWASHIN' THEM.

YOU ACCUSE MY PARTNER?
NO, WE TAKE HIM NOW.
TIME ENOUGH FOR TALK WHEN WE GET HIM TO OA.
LET HIM SPEAK...

I SAW GREEN MAN WHEN YOU MADE ME COME HERE, VATH.
I DON'T SPOOK EASY, BUT HE WAS ACTING REAL STRANGE. I DECIDED RIGHT THEN I DIDN'T WANT TO SPEAK TO MOGO.
IF THERE IS DANGER HERE, WE MUST AT LEAST GIVE THE HONOR LANTERN A HEARING.

YOU ALL KNOW ME. I'M NO TREEHUGGER. NEVER NEEDED MOGO'S HELP--BUT I KNOW HOW HE WORKS. SHOWS YOU WHAT'S TROUBLIN' YOU AND HELPS MAKE SENSE OF IT.
BUT NOT THIS TIME. MOGO REACHED INTO MY MIND--PULLED OUT NIGHTMARES I HAVEN'T HAD FOR YEARS.
FELT LIKE I WAS LOSING MY MARBLES...

...ALMOST-- AND I MEAN ALMOST-- FELT... AFRAID.

IS THAT IT?
NO. THERE ARE GLOWING... INSECTS SWARMING AROUND IN THERE. THEY CAME FOR ME.
I JUST GOT A SHIELD UP IN TIME.
I'M GUESSIN' OTHER LANTERNS WHO'VE BEEN HERE WEREN'T SO QUICK. LIKE TANAKATA Z, FR'INSTANCE.

INSECTS? IN A FOREST? YOU DON'T SAY.
I KNOW ALL THE INSECT RACES THAT THRIVE IN MOGO'S GREEN. MANY ARE DISTANT COUSINS OF MINE.
LET ME TAKE A LOOK.

HAH. THESE ARE NOT INSECTS. THEY ARE SPORES. FUNGAL SPORES.
IN ALL MY YEARS, I HAVE NEVER ENCOUNTERED THEM HERE BEFORE.
THEY MUST BE FROM OFF-WORLD. MAYBE MOGO HAS SOME KIND OF SPACE-BORNE DISEASE.

PROVES NOTHING, GARDNER. CERTAINLY NOT YOUR THEORY THAT TANAKATA Z WAS BRAINWASHED AND KILLED HIS PARTNER AND HIMSELF TO FRAME YOU.
WE HAVE TO GET THIS...THIS INFECTION EXAMINED BY EXPERTS.
WE SURE DO. THAT'S WHY I CALLED THE DOCTOR--

THIS BETTER BE GOOD, GARDNER. I'VE GOT A HOME PLANET THAT NEEDS MY URGENT ATTENTION.
YEAH, WE KNOW KORUGAR'S A PRETTY SICK PLACE, NATU--
--BUT RIGHT NOW, MOGO'S EVEN SICKER.

MOGO SICK? WHAT DO YOU MEAN?
THERE'S SOME KINDA ALIEN FUNGUS IN HIS FORESTS.
LANTERNS WHO COME TO GET THEIR HEADS STRAIGHT LEAVE WITH 'EM TURNED INSIDE OUT.

I--I'VE SEEN THESE SPORES BEFORE. LAST TIME I WAS HERE.
YEAH? NOTICE ANYTHING ELSE THEN?

ONLY TANAKATA Z BEING HIS USUAL CREEPY--
HMM. THIS IS FUNGAL, ALL RIGHT. BIOCHEM'S NOT NATIVE AND THERE'S UNUSUAL NEURAL ENERGY.

SPORES SPREAD BY GROWING, THEN JOINING INTO A COHERENT MASS THAT PRODUCES NEW SPORES.
SOMEWHERE IN HERE MUST BE THAT MOTHER-SPORE.

--HALLUCINATIONS.

OLD GHOSTS

DAVE GIBBONS writer PATRICK GLEASON penciller
PRENTISS ROLLINS & TOM NGUYEN inkers
MOOSE BAUMANN colorist PHIL BALSMAN letterer

BE WARNED, ITS NEURAL CHARGE WILL BE VERY HIGH. QUITE CAPABLE OF PRODUCING--

STICK TOGETHER AND...

KEEP YOUR... SHIELDS UP!

IF YA MAKE CONTACT WITH THE... SPORES, YOU'LL...BE SEEING THESE NIGHTMARES... FOREVER.
YOU'RE... RIGHT. INSIDE THE BODY...THE NEURAL DISRUPTION WOULD BE... IMPOSSIBLE TO RESIST.
YOU'RE... NOT... REAL!
I'M NOT SOME... HATCHLING, SCARED OF... GHOSTS.
NOT... AFRAID.

JUST TRICKS OF... THE LIGHT.
BUT OUR LANTERN LIGHT IS STRONGER!
GARDNER, YOU KNOW SOMEONE WHO'S BEEN EXPOSED TO THE SPORES? IF SO, I WANT TO EXAMINE THEM.
ONE FOR SURE, BUT HE'S DEAD NOW. OUR FRIEND TANAKATA Z.
I'LL ACCESS CENTRAL RECORDS ON OA--GET A LIST OF LANTERNS WHO'VE BEEN ON MOGO RECENTLY.
GOOD.
MEANWHILE, I NEED TO SEE WHAT WE'RE DEALING WITH HERE ON THE GROUND.
THERE IT IS-- A HUGE FUNGAL MASS, SPREADING UNDER MOGO'S GREENERY.
WE HAVE TO FIND THE CENTER OF IT AND DESTROY IT.
OA'S ONLINE.
MOST RECENT VISITORS HERE ARE GREEN MAN, TANAKATA Z AND--

KILOWOG!

KOOM!
SKOOM
GARDNER. I'M HERE TA PUNISH YOU FOR MURDER.
OUTTA THE WAY, TRAITORS. I'LL DEAL WITH YOUSE NEXT.
MURDER? WHAT IS THIS, GARDNER?
LATER, DOC. FOR NOW, JUST TAKE A LOOK AT HIM AND TAKE A LOOK AT ME, AND TELL ME--
--WHICH OF US LOOKS MAD ENOUGH TO KILL SOMEONE?
WE'RE WITH GARDNER.
WE'LL HOLD KILOWOG OFF. BUY YOU SOME TIME.
GNNAAH!
ALL RIGHT. LET'S GET TO THE ROOT OF THIS!

WHAT?
YOU DEFEND A MURDERER?
THEN YOU DESERVE THE SAME FATE.
DEATH!

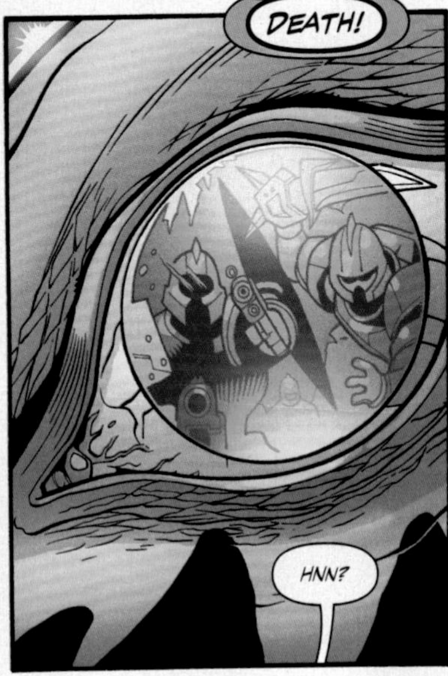
HNN?

STAY WITH ME, ISAMOT. AND KEEP YOUR SHIELD UP, DAMMIT!
YEAH. OKAY, OKAY.
YOU ROOKIES DON'T STAND A CHANCE AGAINST ME. I TAUGHT YOU EVERYTHING YOU KNOW.

AND I HAVE THE POWER OF ALL BOLOVAX.
I AM ALL BOLOVAX NOW.
HOW CAN YOU STAND AGAINST THE POWER OF A PLANET?

WE NEED TO CUT OUT THE DISEASE.
COMPLETELY.
IT--IT'S BIGGER THAN I IMAGINED. WE HAVE TO CONTAIN ITS BOUNDARY.
WE'LL NEED THE OTHERS.
YOU GET DOCTORING HERE AND I'LL GO TRY TO PACIFY THE POOZER.
HONOR LANTERN GARDNER...
I AM SMALL, BUT MY VENOM CAN STOP A THUNGORONIAN IRONBEAST.
THE CORRECT DOSE WOULD CERTAINLY STOP SENIOR LANTERN KILOWOG.
WAIT. I'LL COME TOO. IF I CAN EXAMINE KILOWOG, I'LL UNDERSTAND THIS THING BETTER.
AND IF I'M ABLE TO CURE HIM, HE CAN ADD HIS POWER TO OURS.
ALL RIGHT. LET'S GO, MCFLY.

PAH! I TAUGHT YOU GRUNTS WELL--
--BUT EVEN TOGETHER YOU'RE STILL NO MATCH FOR ME.
OOF!
SKRAKK
DAMMIT! CAN'T GET PAST HIS DEFENSES.
WE NEED THE OTHERS, VATH. ATTACK FROM ALL SIDES.
YOU GOT IT, LIZARD BOY!
MUTINY!
YOU WILL NEVER HOLD ME--

WE GOT HIM, BZZD.
DO YOUR STING THING--AND HURRY!

BZZZZZZZZ

SNIK
CHAAAH!

you will all pay for...

KEEP A SHIELD AROUND HIM.
STOP RE-INFECTION.

YOU SURE YOU KNOW WHAT YOU'RE DOIN', POKING AROUND IN HIS HEAD, RED?
A WALL FULL OF DIPLOMAS SURE, GARDNER.
YES. IT'S HERE. DEEP IN HIS BRAIN. I JUST NEED TO--
HRRHNNN RRHNNHH!
WHAT IN THE SEVEN HELLS IS THAT?
BLAST IT!
YOU CANNOT EXCISSSE USSS ALL.
MOGO BELONGSSS TO SSSIN--

NNOOOOOOO...
KILOWOG OKAY?
HE WILL BE.
HE'S REGAINING CONSCIOUSNESS.
BZZD'S DOSE OF VENOM WAS WELL JUDGED.
MY FRIENDS.
MOGO?
WONDERED WHEN WE'D HEAR FROM YOU, BIG BOY.
BEEN BUSY. NO TIME FOR TALK.
NOW YOU MUST LEAVE.
IT BURROWS DEEPER. TOWARDS MY CORE. IT SEEKS TO INFECT ME, TOO.
ISN'T MOGO ALREADY INFECTED, LANTERN GARDNER?
KEEP UP, PAL. AS LONG AS THE FUNGUS STAYED ON THE SURFACE, IT WAS NO MORE THAN A ZIT TO A PLANET THIS SIZE.
IT COULD DO THE DIRTY WITHOUT MOGO EVEN NOTICING.
BUT IF THE SPORES REACH MOGO'S CORE...

WE NEED TO PREVENT THAT. WE HAVE TO CUT, AND CUT DEEP.
NO TIME. LEAVE. NOW.
LEAVE? HAS IT SENT YOU MAD ALREADY, MOGO?
NO. NOT MAD. I WILL DEAL.
YOU? HOW?
HEADS UP, TROOPS.
I HAVE MOVED MY ORBIT INTO THE PATH OF AN ASTEROID.
ITS IMPACT WILL DESTROY THE EVIL. BURN IT OUT. FOREVER.
LEAVE.
NOW.
YOU HEARD THE BIG GREEN MARBLE!
LET'S FLY!

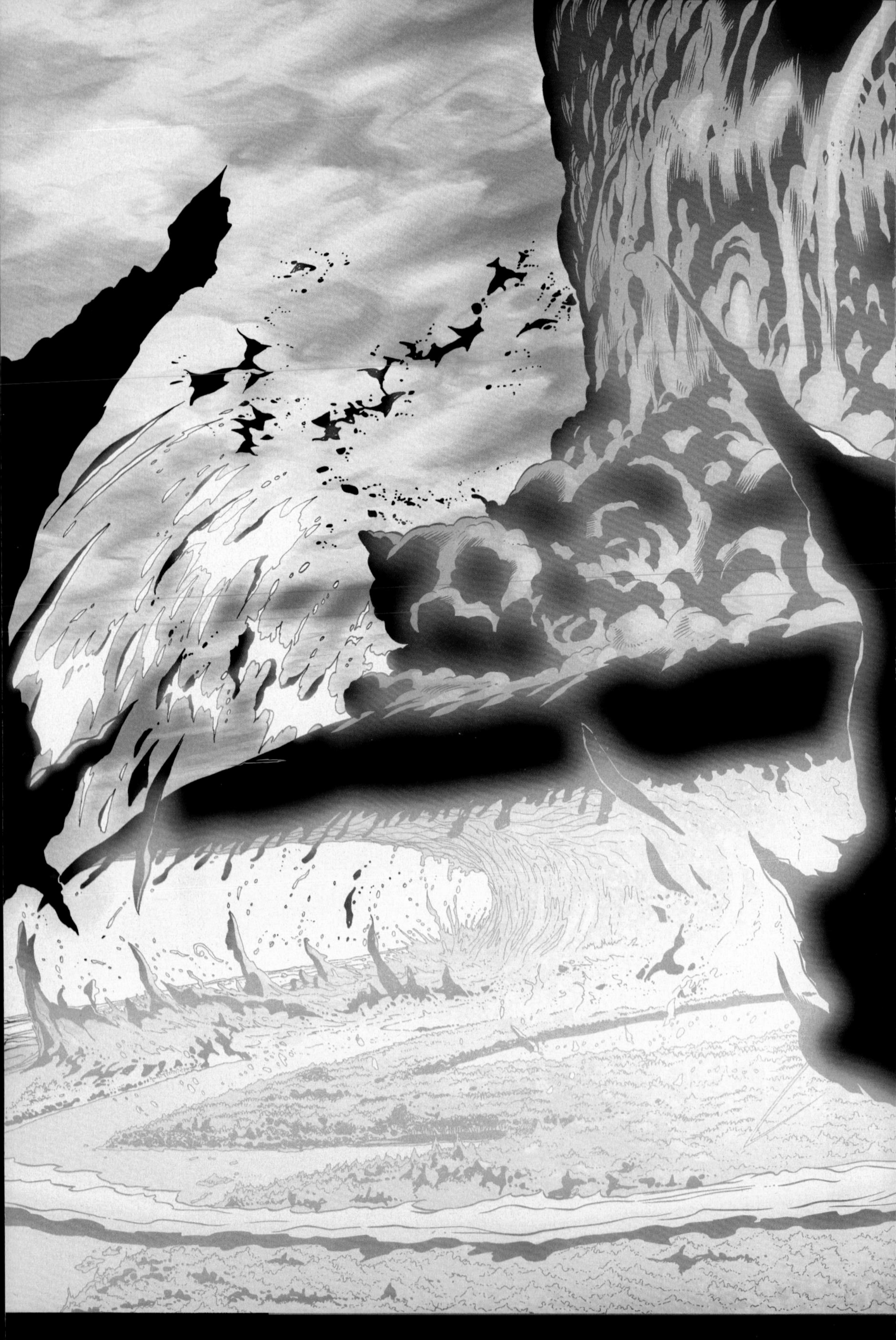

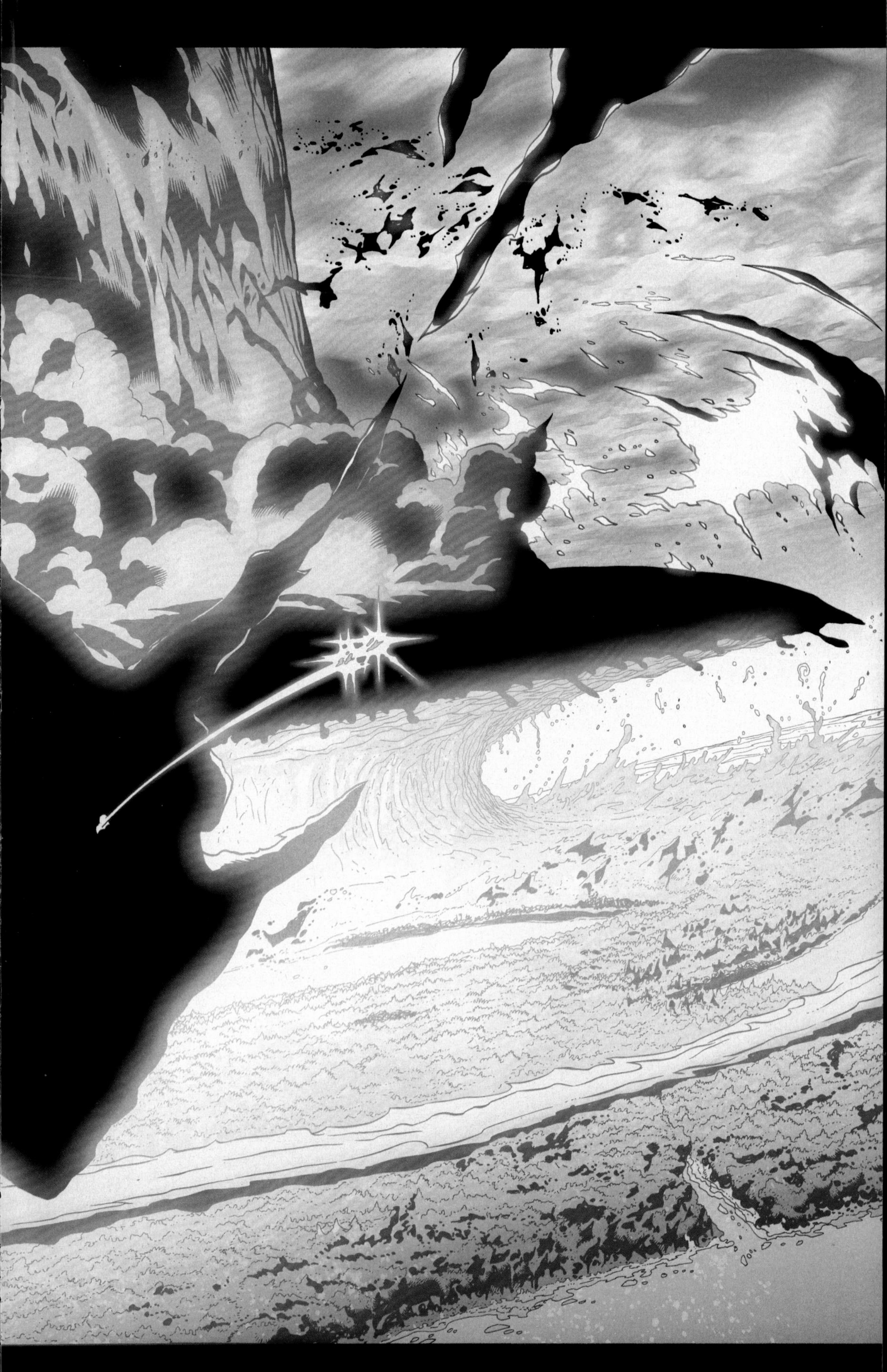

OA
PLANETARY CITADEL OF THE GUARDIANS OF THE UNIVERSE.
THE SCANS SHOW THEY ARE ALL CLEAR.
LANTERN NATU'S MEDICAL OPINION WAS CORRECT.
THE DESTRUCTION OF THE CENTRAL MASS CUT THE NEURAL ENERGY SUPPLY TO THE INDIVIDUAL INFESTATIONS, AND THEY WITHERED AWAY.

HOWEVER, WHAT REMAINS UNEXPLAINED IS THE SOURCE OF THIS ATTACK ON MOGO AND THE CORPS.
WE LOST GOOD LANTERNS.

THERE WAS PLANNING AND MALEVOLENCE BEHIND THIS.
AND I NEARLY GOT FRAMED FOR MURDER, REMEMBER?
YEAH, IT'S GOTTA BE MORE THAN MOGO CATCHIN' SOME KINDA COSMIC HEAD-COLD...

I KILLED HIM, KILOWOG. I KILLED MY PARTNER, STEL.

CAN I EVER BE FORGIVEN?

NO ONE BLAMES YOU, GREEN MAN. LEAST OF ALL ME.

I WAS OUTTA CONTROL, TOO.

SORRY WE DOUBTED YOU, LANTERN GARDNER.

WE HAD TO DO OUR DUTY.

NO SWEAT, AMIGOS. I'D HAVE DONE THE SAME.

ONLY DIFFERENCE IS, I'D HAVE PUT YOUR ASSES IN THE BRIG BEFORE YOU COULD EVEN BLINK.

SECTOR 2261.
MOGO.
THE INFECTION IS GONE, LANTERN NATU?
I'VE CHECKED RIGHT DOWN TO THE BEDROCK. THE HEAT OF THE IMPACT STERILIZED EVERYTHING.
IT'S GONE, LANTERN BZZD.
SORANIK NATU.
PLEASE STAY. YOU ARE TIRED. LET ME HELP.
THANK YOU, MOGO, BUT YOU HAVE SCARS OF YOUR OWN...
BESIDES, KORUGAR CALLS ME.
I WILL WATCH OVER MY SECTOR PARTNER UNTIL HIS WOUNDS ARE HEALED.
I KNOW YOU WILL, LITTLE BROTHER.
TAKE CARE.
WE MUST ALL BE VIGILANT.

LIKE GOOD, EVIL COMES IN EVERY SHAPE AND SIZE.